THE FRENCH CANADIANS

The Peoples of North America

THE FRENCH CANADIANS

Nancy Wartik

CHELSEA HOUSE PUBLISHERS

New York   Philadelphia

On the cover: Shortly after World War I, *habitants* gather outside their homestead in northern Quebec.

CHELSEA HOUSE PUBLISHERS
Editor-in-Chief: Nancy Toff
Executive Editor: Remmel T. Nunn
Managing Editor: Karyn Gullen Browne
Copy Chief: Juliann Barbato
Picture Editor: Adrian G. Allen
Art Director: Maria Epes
Manufacturing Manager: Gerald Levine

The Peoples of North America
Senior Editor: Sam Tanenhaus

Staff for THE FRENCH CANADIANS
Assistant Editor: Abigail Meisel
Copy Editor: Karen Hammonds
Deputy Copy Chief: Ellen Scordato
Editorial Assistant: Elizabeth Nix
Picture Research: PAR/NYC and Barbara Schultz
Assistant Art Director: Laurie Jewell
Senior Designer: Noreen M. Lamb
Layout: Louise Lippin
Production Coordinator: Joseph Romano
Cover Illustration: Paul Biniasz
Banner Design: Hrana L. Janto

3 5 7 9 8 6 4 2

Library of Congress Cataloging-in-Publication Data

Wartik, Nancy.
  The French Canadians.

  (The Peoples of North America)
  Bibliography: p.
  Includes index.
  1. French-Canadians—Juvenile literature.
I. Title. II. Series.
F1027.W37 1989   971'.004114   88-25648
ISBN 0-87754-879-X
    0-7910-0264-0 (pbk.)

CONTENTS

THE PEOPLES OF NORTH AMERICA

CHELSEA HOUSE PUBLISHERS

A
NATION
OF
NATIONS

Daniel Patrick Moynihan

The Constitution of the United States begins: "We the People of the United States . . ." Yet, as we know, the United States is not made up of a single group of people. It is made up of many peoples. Immigrants from Europe, Asia, Africa, and Central and South America settled in North America seeking a new life filled with opportunities unavailable in their homeland. Coming from many nations, they forged one nation and made it their own. More than 100 years ago, Walt Whitman expressed this perception of America as a melting pot: "Here is not merely a nation, but a teeming Nation of nations."

Although the ingenuity and acts of courage of these immigrants, our ancestors, shaped the North American way of life, we sometimes take their contributions for granted. This fine series, *The Peoples of North America*, examines the experiences and contributions of the immigrants and how these contributions determined the future of the United States and Canada.

Immigrants did not abandon their ethnic traditions when they reached the shores of North America. Each ethnic group had its own customs and traditions, and each brought different experiences, accomplishments, skills, values, styles of dress, and tastes in food that lingered long after its arrival. Yet this profusion of differences created a singularity, or bond, among the immigrants.

The United States and Canada are unusual in this respect. Whereas religious and ethnic differences have sparked intolerance throughout the rest of the world—from the 17th-century religious wars to the 19th-century nationalist movements in Europe to the near extermination of the Jewish people under Nazi Germany—North Americans have struggled to learn how to respect each other's differences and live in harmony.

Millions of immigrants from scores of homelands brought diversity to our continent. In a mass migration, some 12 million immigrants passed through the waiting rooms of New York's Ellis Island; thousands more came to the West Coast. At first, these immigrants were welcomed because labor was needed to meet the demands of the Industrial Age. Soon, however, the new immigrants faced the prejudice of earlier immigrants who saw them as a burden on the economy. Legislation was passed to limit immigration. The Chinese Exclusion Act of 1882 was among the first laws closing the doors to the promise of America. The Japanese were also effectively excluded by this law. In 1924, Congress set immigration quotas on a country-by-country basis.

Such prejudices might have triggered war, as they did in Europe, but North Americans chose negotiation and compromise, instead. This determination to resolve differences peacefully has been the hallmark of the peoples of North America.

The remarkable ability of Americans to live together as one people was seriously threatened by the issue of slavery. It was a symptom of growing intolerance in the world. Thousands of settlers from the British Isles had arrived in the colonies as indentured servants, agreeing to work for a specified number of years on farms or as apprentices in return for passage to America and room and board. When the first Africans arrived in the then-British colonies during the 17th century, some colonists thought that they too should be treated as indentured servants. Eventually, the question of whether the Africans should be viewed as indentured, like the English, or as slaves who could be owned for life, was considered in a Maryland court. The court's calamitous decree held that blacks were slaves bound to lifelong servitude, and so were their children.

America went through a time of moral examination and civil war before it finally freed African slaves and their descendants. The principle that all people are created equal had faced its greatest challenge and survived.

Yet the court ruling that set blacks apart from other races fanned flames of discrimination that burned long after slavery was abolished—and that still flicker today. The concept of racism had existed for centuries in countries throughout the world. For instance, when the Manchus conquered China in the 13th century, they decreed that Chinese and Manchus could not intermarry. To impress their superiority on the conquered Chinese, the Manchus ordered all Chinese men to wear their hair in a long braid called a queue.

By the 19th century, some intellectuals took up the banner of racism, citing Charles Darwin. Darwin's scientific studies hypothesized that highly evolved animals were dominant over other animals. Some advocates of this theory applied it to humans, asserting that certain races were more highly evolved than others and thus were superior.

This philosophy served as the basis for a new form of discrimination, not only against nonwhite people but also against various ethnic groups. Asians faced harsh discrimination and were depicted by popular 19th-century newspaper cartoonists as depraved, degenerate, and deficient in intelligence. When the Irish flooded American cities to escape the famine in Ireland, the cartoonists caricatured the typical "Paddy" (a common term for Irish immigrants) as an apelike creature with jutting jaw and sloping forehead.

By the 20th century, racism and ethnic prejudice had given rise to virulent theories of a Northern European master race. When Adolf Hitler came to power in Germany in 1933, he popularized the notion of Aryan supremacy. "Aryan," a term referring to the Indo-European races, was applied to so-called superior physical characteristics such as blond hair, blue eyes, and delicate facial features. Anyone with darker and heavier features was considered inferior. Buttressed by these theories, the German Nazi state from

1933 to 1945 set out to destroy European Jews, along with Poles, Russians, and other groups considered inferior. It nearly succeeded. Millions of these people were exterminated.

The tragedies brought on by ethnic and racial intolerance throughout the world demonstrate the importance of North America's efforts to create a society free of prejudice and inequality.

A relatively recent example of the New World's desire to resolve ethnic friction nonviolently is the solution the Canadians found to a conflict between two ethnic groups. A long-standing dispute as to whether Canadian culture was properly English or French resurfaced in the mid-1960s, dividing the peoples of the French-speaking Quebec Province from those of the English-speaking provinces. Relations grew tense, then bitter, then violent. The Royal Commission on Bilingualism and Biculturalism was established to study the growing crisis and to propose measures to ease the tensions. As a result of the commission's recommendations, all official documents and statements from the national government's capital at Ottawa are now issued in both French and English, and bilingual education is encouraged.

The year 1980 marked a coming of age for the United States's ethnic heritage. For the first time, the U.S. Census asked people about their ethnic background. Americans chose from more than 100 groups, including French Basque, Spanish Basque, French Canadian, Afro-American, Peruvian, Armenian, Chinese, and Japanese. The ethnic group with the largest response was English (49.6 million). More than 100 million Americans claimed ancestors from the British Isles, which includes England, Ireland, Wales, and Scotland. There were almost as many Germans (49.2 million) as English. The Irish-American population (40.2 million) was third, but the next largest ethnic group, the Afro-Americans, was a distant fourth (21 million). There was a sizable group of French ancestry (13 million), as well as of Italian (12 million). Poles, Dutch, Swedes, Norwegians, and Russians followed. These groups, and other smaller ones, represent the wondrous profusion of ethnic influences in North America.

Canada, too, has learned more about the diversity of its population. Studies conducted during the French/English conflict showed that Canadians were descended from Ukrainians, Germans, Italians, Chinese, Japanese, native Indians, and Eskimos, among others. Canada found it had no ethnic majority, although nearly half of its immigrant population had come from the British Isles. Canada, like the United States, is a land of immigrants for whom mutual tolerance is a matter of reason as well as principle.

The people of North America are the descendants of one of the greatest migrations in history. And that migration is not over. Koreans, Vietnamese, Nicaraguans, Cubans, and many others are heading for the shores of North America in large numbers. This mix of cultures shapes every aspect of our lives. To understand ourselves, we must know something about our diverse ethnic ancestry. Nothing so defines the North American nations as the motto on the Great Seal of the United States: *E Pluribus Unum*—Out of Many, One. 〜

In July 1967, French president Charles de Gaulle made headlines when he endorsed Quebec's Separatist movement.

WHO ARE THE FRENCH CANADIANS?

The year was 1967 and the place was Montreal, Canada. Beneath the balcony of the Hôtel de Ville, Montreal's city hall, a crowd of half a million thronged the streets. It was the nation's centennial and leaders from around the world were attending its celebration. The French-speaking residents of Quebec province, the Quebecois, eagerly awaited the appearance of a special guest: French president Charles de Gaulle.

This was a time of upheaval and change for the Quebecois. They felt a rekindling of pride—long dormant—in their French heritage. De Gaulle, a leader respected around the world, represented their tie to their ancestral past. At last he stepped onto the balcony to address the crowd, which gave him a rousing welcome. He stretched out his arms and began an emotional speech, touching on the long-standing link between Quebec and France, once Canada's mother country. Then, in an impassioned outburst, de Gaulle declared, "Vive Montréal! Vive le Québec libre!"—Long live Montreal! Long live free Quebec!

The words, like a spark applied to dry tinder, ignited the crowd into wild applause. De Gaulle's words referred to separatism, a movement—relatively new in 1967—that called for Quebec to become an independent nation, divided politically from the rest of Canada. The highly controversial movement had already resulted in episodes of violence. The renowned French president's call for a "free" Quebec endorsed this idea and lent it new credibility. De Gaulle's words quickly earned him a rebuke from Canada's prime minister, Lester Pearson, and de Gaulle immediately departed the country in a huff. Still, he had started a snowball rolling downhill.

De Gaulle's rallying cry marked a turning point for the Separatist movement, itself the offshoot of a call for reform that began in Quebec in 1960. By 1970, an amazing 41 percent of Quebecois believed the province could survive without the rest of Canada.

Separatism provoked a national crisis that rocked the whole country to its foundations. The impact of the movement altered everything, from the way Canadian products were labeled and the design of the nation's flag (in 1964–65), to the country's school curricula and its treatment of minorities. Other Canadians—includ-

In January 1965, Canada began production of a new flag that replaced the English Union Jack with a maple leaf.

ing many of French origin—often rejected the Separatist aims of Quebec. They complained that the Quebec French were like "spoiled children," throwing tantrums because they could not get their own way.

Who were the Quebecois and what had led them to contemplate a move so drastic as seceding from the rest of Canada? How could a fraction of the country—less than a quarter—wrest important concessions from the majority? And why did the French Canadians think they differed so markedly from the inhabitants of another province, such as British Columbians?

These questions defy simple explanation, though some clues lie in the French Canadians' remarkable 400-year-long history. It is the history of a people whose loyalty to mother tongue, ethnic roots, and religious faith has hardly been matched by any other European minority living in North America. The story of French Canada has been described by scholar Mason Wade as "perhaps the most colorful, for its span of years, of any human record." Reverence for their past has been a potent force in the phenomenon of French-Canadian survival. Quebec pride is on display even on the license plates issued to every car registered in the province. The plates bear the motto *Je me souviens* (I remember).

The French Canadians constitute the largest single group of Francophones (French speakers) in the Anglophone (English-speaking) population of North America. This community includes a wide diversity of Canadians. The most prominent are the more than 5 million residents of Quebec (81 percent of the province), who, according to the 1986 Canadian census, grew up speaking and still know the French tongue. In the western province of Manitoba, some areas are still predominantly French-speaking. And in Canada's Maritime Provinces in the east—Nova Scotia, Prince Edward Island, and especially New Brunswick—15 percent of the 1.7 million residents grew up speaking French. Of the total Canadian population of about 25 million, roughly one-quarter is of French descent.

By 1965, when this demonstration occurred, separatism had grown into a large-scale movement.

But their French identity is only one of several that continue to influence the Quebecois. They also are the inheritors of a pioneer tradition: Their ancestors were among the first Europeans to tame the vast Canadian wilderness. It is important to remember that French Canadians are not identical to the French. Although the Quebec flag flies the *fleur-de-lis*, or iris, that has symbolized France for hundreds of years, the province's literature, traditions, and popular culture differ from those of France. In fact, some Frenchmen snobbishly regard French Canadians as unsophisticated "country cousins," speakers of *joual*, a dialect Parisians consider vulgar. Visitors from France find Quebec, at first glance, much more North American than European.

Quebec, not France, is the French-Canadian homeland and the place where this group's strongest allegiance lies. It is the second most populous province after Ontario and also the largest in total area, indeed larger than any of the 50 United States. French is the language of government and of most schools and businesses. The province's leading urban center, the cosmopolitan city of Montreal, is two-thirds French-speaking, and its second major city, Quebec City, is 97 percent French-speaking. For other French Canadians, Quebec has been a political inspiration; as Quebec has gone, so, in many instances, have French-Canadian communities across Canada.

Yet despite Quebec's venerable heritage and its economic and political strength, its history over the past 200 years has been marred by an ugly pattern of discrimination and prejudice. The end of the British Conquest of 1763, in which the French lost the war for control of Canada, launched a struggle between Francophones and Anglophones. In the years to come, the French would find themselves strangers in their own land, fighting for power in the face of a dominant English-Canadian nationality.

This bitter conflict did much to unite French Canadians, but at the same time it created among them a sense of inferiority. The Protestant British referred dis-

In this photo of Quebec City (circa 1900) the elegant Chateau Fontenac looms above a street crowded with charming shops. In 1988, 97 percent of the city's population was Francophone.

dainfully to Catholic Quebec as "the priest-ridden province." Even in recent decades, French who publicly used their own tongue might be ordered to "speak white" by British who overheard them. In the mid-1980s, Francophone Canadians still earned on average 22 percent less than Anglophones.

For hundreds of years, French Canadians were stereotyped as devout but backward peasants who lacked education and ambition. Their primary values—religious faith, home, family, community, and a way of life incorporating longtime traditions—were often dismissed contemptuously by an English-speaking society that emphasized wealth, education, and power.

Facts and figures have their place in a portrait of the French Canadians, but it is important to remember the impact that 200 years of discrimination, oppression, and poverty has had on their culture and character. This history was a key factor in the turbulence of recent decades, and it explains much about who the French Canadians are today. ❧

This map of New France (Canada), published in 1547, shows how the area looked to the first Europeans who saw it. The figures with drawn bows represent Indian communities. The explorer depicted in the foreground is probably Jacques Cartier.

NEW FRANCE AND THE AGE OF EXPLORATION

The early history of Canada is the history of its explorers and colonists.

They were Europeans who set sail for the New World during the Renaissance, the sudden flowering of literature, science, art, and exploration that began in Italy in the 14th century.

It was during this era—in 1492, in fact—that the Italian mariner Christopher Columbus happened upon a new continent across the Atlantic Ocean. His discovery prompted further expeditions. Soon vessels returned from long voyages laden with rare spices or—even more to the liking of European governments—gold and silver. Nations vied to stake first claim to the treasures of distant lands. And navigators dreamed of finding a "northwest passage," a quick water route to the legendary riches of Asia. Mariners who searched for this elusive passage stumbled onto several territories, and one of them was Canada.

The rulers and merchants of France wanted to share in all this foreign wealth. In 1524 King Francis I com-

In 1524, explorer Giovanni (or, in Latin, Janus) da Verrazano reached the eastern coast of North America and proceeded as far north as Newfoundland.

missioned Giovanni da Verrazano, a well-traveled Italian navigator, to sail west under the French flag. He reached the eastern coast of America and then pressed northward as far as present-day Newfoundland. Thereafter, the French referred to the North American Atlantic coast as New France—a name the French colony in Canada would bear for almost 250 years.

In 1528 Verrazano attempted a return journey to New France but met an unhappy fate. Exactly what happened is unknown, though it is generally believed he was devoured by cannibals in the West Indies. King Francis I next commissioned Jacques Cartier to seek a route to the Far East. In the spring of 1534 Cartier reached the jagged east coast of Canada. He and his men did not find the northwest passage, but they did discover "as fine a land as it is possible to see, being very fertile and covered with magnificent trees" and abundantly supplied with wild animals, fish, birds, fruits, and flowers of every description. The explorers also encountered Indians eager to barter the furs they wore for metalware, beads, and trinkets.

The Indians whetted Cartier's interest with descriptions of a kingdom to the west "where lie infinite gold, rubies, and other riches." They called it the land of the Saguenay. But on a second trip to New France, the explorer located no magical kingdom. Instead he discovered the St. Lawrence River, a mighty waterway that ran the length of what is now southern Quebec province.

Along the banks of the river, Cartier came upon Iroquois Indian villages on the sites of what are now Quebec City and Montreal. At the second site, a well-designed town of some 1,000 inhabitants, the Iroquois led him to the foot of the low mountain on and around which today's city stands. Cartier named this hill Mont Royal (Royal Mountain), from which the name Montreal derives. Legend has it that Cartier also gave Canada its name. When he asked the Indians what they called their country, he made a wide gesture meant to

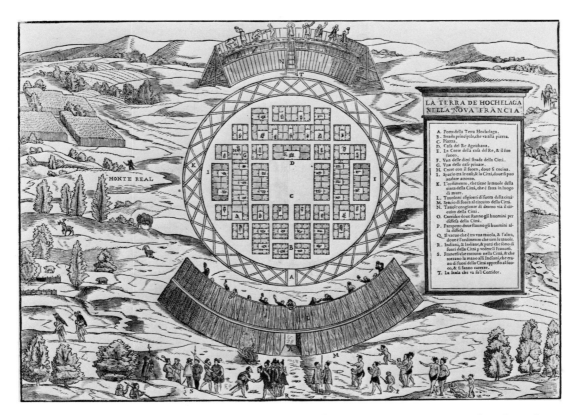

encompass the entire land. The Indians thought he was pointing specifically to their own home and spoke the name *Kanata*—probably a word for village. Cartier used this word to refer to the small region around Quebec, and as the territory expanded the name took in more and more land.

Cartier never found the land of the Saguenay, and the barrels full of gold and diamonds that he brought back to France from a third trip turned out to be "fool's gold" (pyrite) and quartz. Cartier did not realize that Canada's true fortune lay in its more mundane resources—trees, game, and rivers.

But another explorer, Samuel de Champlain, knew better. He set out for the New World in 1603, some 70 years after Cartier. Champlain was enchanted by New France and the unlimited potential of its rugged, spacious terrain. He made the remarkable total of 23 cross-

A Venetian woodcut from the mid-16th century shows the city plan of Montreal and its surrounding landscape. The arc at the bottom (A) indicates the entrance to the city, where settlers greet Indian men and women.

ings between old and New France—no simple undertaking in those days of small, wooden sailing ships. Every journey involved great risk. The voyage could take up to three months, ships were frequently lost at sea, and passengers—even hardy sailors—often succumbed to diseases caused by the poor diet and unsanitary conditions on board.

Champlain was not content merely to explore Canada. He made unceasing efforts to start and maintain a colony and distinguished himself as a diplomat, politician, writer, artist, builder, mapmaker, botanist, and gardener, as well as an explorer, sailor, and fighter. In 1608 he founded Quebec City.

Until the end of his life, Champlain still hoped to find a route to China, but this vision did not slow his efforts to tap the great potential of Canada itself. Today he is considered the "father of Canada." He witnessed, for one thing, the growing Canadian fur trade, which proved very profitable for France. During the 16th century, fishermen who had gone to Newfoundland to plumb its teeming waters began to barter with the Indians—exchanging cloth, knives, needles, earrings,

mirrors, and other knickknacks for the pelts of elk, moose, wolf, lynx, and other animals.

Furs were exotic curiosities in Europe, and soon something called the beaver hat came into fashion on the Continent. These hats were made in various styles, but they all used beaver fur. Once the hats became the rage, the demand for Canadian beaver fur surged. Beaver furs remained an economic mainstay in Canada through the mid-1800s—and the country is still known for the quality of its furs.

Trading was only one of Champlain's reasons for wanting to colonize New France. Champlain lived during a time of bitter rivalry waged in Europe between Catholics and Protestants. At issue were the guiding principles of Christianity, which were fiercely debated as part of a 16th-century movement known as the Reformation. Like many of his compatriots, Champlain fervently believed Indians must be baptized "to a knowledge of God" in the *Catholic* faith.

French Catholic leaders agreed that the Church should be a presence in New France, where some 200,000 Indians might be won over to Catholicism. Nuns and priests sailed to New World settlements. They established the colony's first hospitals and schools and were very often leaders in the community. Of the missionaries who traveled to the wilderness to convert far-flung Indian tribes, many bravely died as martyrs— tortured to death by hostile Indians.

The courage and strength of will the nuns and clergy displayed became an enduring legend in French-Canadian history, and until quite recently their influence among their people remained unusually strong. Without the unceasing efforts of the Church, the colony might have faltered.

The French Crown gave only minimal support to its colonies. Of more pressing concern were the bitter religious wars of the Reformation and the battles France often waged in Europe. As a result, French kings were usually content to grant "monopolies" to select nobles or groups of merchants, who thus gained exclusive rights to the Canadian fur trade and to colonization.

Samuel de Champlain—"the father of Canada"—crossed the Atlantic Ocean 23 times. In 1608 he founded Quebec, one of his many long-lasting achievements.

Jesuit missionaries go calmly to the stake in this 1648 engraving.

Thus, Champlain acted alone to spur interest in and support for New France. He wrote and illustrated half a dozen books on its wonders and curiosities—its plants and animals and its "savages," as the French called the Indians. He begged for funding for his colonizing schemes from the king or from merchants. And he realized immediately that to extend the exploration of New France and to expand the fur trade, he would have to learn the ways of the wilderness from the Indians. Champlain befriended the Algonquian, Montagnais, and Huron, several times helping them battle their common enemy, the Iroquois. Unfortunately his diplomatic efforts helped sow the seeds of a long-standing, bitter hostility between the French and the Iroquois.

The first colonization effort in which Champlain was involved was in Acadia, a name that in the 17th and 18th centuries referred to what are now the provinces of Nova Scotia, New Brunswick, and Prince Edward Island, as well as parts of Maine and Quebec. Champlain was one of some 80 men anchored for the winter on a tiny island off the New Brunswick coast, hoping to find copper or iron in the area. But when the harsh Canadian winter set in, supplies ran low and 39 men died of scurvy, a disease caused by lack of vitamin C in the diet. In the spring, the colony moved across the bank to Nova Scotia, and the next winter passed more pleasantly. Champlain founded "The Order of Good Cheer" among his men "for to keep us merry," as one reported, and each day a new person was charged with going hunting or fishing to add "some dainty thing" to the meals.

But in 1607, financial and political troubles forced the French king to call a halt to the venture. Later colonization attempts by the French ended abruptly in 1613 when the English attacked and leveled their encampment. From that time on, possession of the region would be constantly disputed by France and England, though a quiet community of French farmers, trappers, and fishermen multiplied through the next century and a half.

In 1608 Champlain returned to New France with 28 men, this time to found a colony along the St. Lawrence. He called the settlement "Kebec," after an Indian word for the spot where a river narrows. But the dread effects of scurvy reduced the number of men to eight by the end of the first winter.

The second winter was better. According to one report, the men's greatest concern was finding ways "to amuse themselves" during the long, cold days and nights. At least one member of the party used his time gainfully. Young Étienne Brûlé, a cocky peasant boy no more than 14 or 15 years old when he came to New France in 1608, learned to speak the tongue of the Montagnais Indians. In 1610, with Brûlé's consent, Champlain sent him off to live with the Algonquians. Brûlé liked his new surroundings so much that he lived among the Indians until his death in 1633. He also learned the Huron and Algonquian languages, served as an interpreter for the Europeans, and became the first European to travel up the Ottawa River. This young man may well have been the first European discoverer of the Great Lakes of Huron, Ontario, Superior, and Erie.

Brûlé himself was among the first of a new breed of French Canadian, much romanticized in the culture's

One of the first coureurs de bois *(woods runners) was Étienne Brûlé, who was in his teens when he left "Kebec" to live among the Indians.*

history. The *coureurs de bois* (literally, "woods runners")—eventually replaced later by *voyageurs* (travelers)—were fur traders who learned the lore of the forest and lived among the Indians to gather furs, returning infrequently to the colony. Fortunately most of them did not come to the same end as Brûlé—after some 20 years among the Indians the natives inexplicably turned on him, chopped him up, and ate him.

Champlain himself died in 1635, just two years after Brûlé; at the time of his death New France was still faltering, especially in comparison to the thriving colonies of the English. By 1627 the colony of Virginia, for example, had some 2,000 settlers, whereas Quebec and Acadia together had only slightly more than 100. In 1663, when all of New France had a total of only 3,000 colonists, 40,000 lived in New England alone.

What kept the numbers of the French colony small? A major factor was the country's main revenue source, the fur trade. It prospered best when its forests were left uncleared; settlements—and the inhabitants they brought—would drive out and slaughter the animals. Thus merchants who held monopolies or territory in Canada usually made little effort to bring over colonists and cultivate the land.

Nor was New France a place for the weak of heart. Those who survived the daunting ocean journey had to face unpredictable natives and scurvy or other disease. The short growing season and the difficulty of getting supplies through the iced-in rivers often resulted in starvation—one year Champlain had to ration the colonists down to seven ounces of ground peas a day.

The climate created other problems. In the 1700s, a Frenchman who spent time in Quebec commented on how "shocking" he found it "not to be able to stir out of doors without being frozen. . . . I have never passed a winter in this country without seeing someone or other carried to the hospital, and who was obliged to have his legs or arms cut off on account of their being benumbed and frozen."

In the century and a half after Quebec was colonized, only some 10,000 people, a tiny number, emigrated there from France. Sometimes beggars from the Parisian streets or convicts imprisoned for lesser crimes were the only colonists who could be rounded up. Although these were certainly not the only people who emigrated, they nonetheless gave the colony an unsavory reputation. Even so, one contemporary asserted that the settlers were "very honest people—of integrity, uprightness, and religion." Many of them were peasants—farmers or laborers—from the northwestern areas of the mother country or artisans, such as carpenters, toolmakers, and bakers.

In the second half of the 17th century, many French soldiers sent to quell Indian uprisings ended up settling in the new colony. Almost all the colonists were Catholics—Protestants were barred early from the colony by royal command. Most colonists were not literate and few had money.

Women came quite early to the colony, although in much smaller numbers than the men. Some of the most heroic figures of French-Canadian history are the nuns and nurses who worked with, taught, and tended to French and Indians alike.

Why did people come? Many heard from friends and neighbors that life in New France was freer, unburdened by the strict taxes and class structure that dominated the old country. They needed only bear in mind that, as colonial governor Pierre Boucher put it, "No people are wanted, either men or women, who cannot turn their hands to some work, unless they are very rich." After several years of hard work, a colonist could make a decent living and possess his own patch of land—a dream out of reach for most French peasants.

But the small population of the colony was a major stumbling block in its development. Not until the 1660s, under the reign of Louis XIV, France's Sun King, was the foundation stone of Canada's future laid more firmly. ✍

NEW FRANCE
BEFORE THE CONQUEST

Early one morning in 1692, a 14-year-old girl named Madeleine de Verchères started down from the fort her father commanded on the St. Lawrence River. She inspected the boats docked at the shore. In the surrounding fields, workers harvested the grain under cool October skies. Madeleine's father, Seigneur François Jarret de Verchères, was on duty as a soldier in Quebec City, and his wife was visiting friends 20 miles away in Montreal.

Suddenly Madeleine heard a shout—the much feared cry that could mean only one thing: Iroquois. They had descended from the woods and seized the field-workers at the harvest. Madeleine turned and ran back to the fort, so closely pursued by one Iroquois that he snatched the scarf from her neck before she ran in and bolted the door. Madeleine was no stranger to Iroquois attacks. She had already lost a brother and two brothers-in-law to them. Only one sentry was on guard at the fort but Madeleine was determined that the Indians not know that. Calling "To arms! To arms!" she ran up the sentry tower and donned a soldier's helmet, trying, as she later wrote, to simulate the noises and gestures a large group of men would make. Then she fired off the cannon to scare the Iroquois and to signal

A French etching depicts an Iroquois outfitted for battle. Colonists soon saw the advantage of wearing snowshoes and took to doing so themselves.

the next fort downriver. The fort fired its cannon in acknowledgment and so the alert was passed fort to fort up to Montreal. Soldiers were dispatched and the de Verchères fort was saved.

For many years, French-Canadian schoolchildren learned this tale of "Canada's youngest heroine." In fact, as time went by the story grew until eventually Madeleine was said to have fended off 45 Iroquois armed with guns before she ever got into the fort and, once inside, to have held them at bay for 8 days.

Her story, one of the few anecdotes we have of early pioneer life in New France, reminds us that in an era when home was a barricaded fort, everyone—no matter what his age or sex—had to be constantly on guard. As one colonist, a nurse who helped found Montreal, remarked, it was common during Indian attacks that "the women, like Amazons, ran out armed like the men, and many times I have seen them in the fight."

Since Champlain's day, the French had gotten along badly with the Iroquois (whose name means "serpent"). A powerful nation, the Iroquois dwelt in an area around Lake Ontario and comprised five tribes. One in particular—the Mohawk ("man-eater") tribe—despised the French and came close to wiping New France off the map. They considered the colonists and their Indian allies rivals in the fur trade that they conducted with English and Dutch settlers.

A French-Canadian priest, describing the difficult situation to a friend back in France, wrote: "One can hardly gather greens in a garden for a salad in safety, and in order to get any supplies of wood everyone has to go in battle order or stand guard. It is not that the Iroquois are always around us, but that one is never sure either that they are there or that they are not, hence we have to beware of them all the time."

The Iroquois were the more dreaded because they frequently carried off their victims and tortured them, usually biting off their fingers to start with and concluding by burning them slowly at the stake. They did not reserve this torture only for whites. The Iroquois' Indian prisoners often died at the stake and took pride in doing so bravely, singing loudly to demonstrate their courage.

Other Indian peoples, including the Huron and the Abenaki, welcomed the arrival of French colonists and made it possible for them to survive in the new land. It was Indians who taught the French how to travel with toboggans and snowshoes when winter made the woods impassable. They taught them how to make and maneuver canoes and how to shoot rapids on the wild St. Lawrence. They introduced them to pumpkins, corn, and squash, and taught them how to cook new meats like moose and beaver and to draw maple syrup from the trees.

The French, unlike the British, responded with equal courtesy. British colonists greatly outnumbered the Indians and—partly because they did not depend on the fur trade for economic survival—blatantly treated Canada's native population as inferiors. The French may have looked down on some of the Indians' customs and beliefs, but they came to know and respect them in a way the British did not. "Most of them have really a nobleness of soul and a constancy of mind at which we rarely arrive, with all the assistance of philosophy and religion," wrote one Frenchman of the Indians he met.

As the Indians came to count on European tools, utensils, and weapons as barter for furs, they stopped relying on their own skills and gradually forgot their old ways. Despite the protests of the clergy, the French traded brandy to the Indians, and alcohol harmed Indian culture. Contact with the French exposed the tribes to new diseases; epidemics of smallpox, influenza, and cholera wiped out thousands of natives. And, caught up in the fur-trade rivalry between the French and the English, the Indians found themselves manipulated by both sides. Their fate in Canada was tragic in many ways, but their influence on the French settlers was strong and lasting.

By the end of the 17th century, New France was still no more populated than a small town in today's Canada or the United States, but Quebec's two major

A woodcut shows a typical Canadian woodsman. Pipe smoking was one of several Indian customs adopted by the colonists.

Montreal, Quebec, circa 1740. A fur-trading post, Montreal was built at the foot of Mont-Royal.

cities had been founded, both along the St. Lawrence, where most of the fertile land lay.

The colonial capital, Quebec City, was perched on the bluffs above the river. A visitor to Quebec City in 1749 noted that the most cultured society on the continent could be found there. And about 125 miles downriver was Montreal, founded in 1642. By the end of the 17th century, many of the streets that still run through "old" Montreal had been laid down, and the colony was a fur-trading outpost.

New France's growth spurt began during the rule of France's flamboyant Sun King, Louis XIV. He dreamed of making France the most powerful kingdom in Europe, and New France fit into those plans. Louis placed much trust in his top minister, or adviser, Jean-Baptiste Colbert. This shrewd and ambitious man realized that once it was developed, New France could yield a steady flow of resources to the mother country. To increase the colony's population, the king's agents rounded up potentially interested emigrants and encouraged them to relocate to the colony. In New France, rather drastic measures were taken to boost its population. Boys were ordered to marry by age 20 and girls by 16. Bachelorhood was made a punishable crime, whereas families with more than 10 children were financially rewarded. Within 20 years, the population had swollen fourfold. The crown also dispatched the soldiers for which New France had long been pleading, to try and quell Iroquois attacks. Colbert also put the energetic Jean Talon in place as colonial "intendant," a position of high authority. Talon encouraged the colonists to be more self-sufficient; soon they were making their own clothes, hats, and shoes instead of spending money to import them from Europe. He also spurred the growth of farming, shipbuilding, and mining.

As the colony grew, daily life slowly assumed a routine pattern. The majority of French Canadians were small farmers, known as habitants, who made a simple living from their small plots of land outside the towns.

New France's social system was basically feudal, with the habitants working the land of the privileged seigneur (lord), but in a country where everyone had to start from scratch, the social distance between the classes mattered much less. A seigneur would settle habitants on his holdings and they would in turn help him clear it of trees and cultivate it. Unlike their French counterparts, the habitants had few yearly taxes to pay.

The landed estates, called *seigneuries*, with a chapel and flour mill that the seigneur built, were self-contained communities. Many villages of Quebec province today still bear the names of the seigneurs who first lived there (Verchères, Madeleine's home, is such a town). On the seigneuries, the habitants dwelt in their small whitewashed homes of wood or stone built low to the ground. In the back was an oven of stone and clay where, once a week, the woman of the house did her baking. The pine furnishings were homemade; colorful woven rugs covered the floors, and pictures of saints decorated the walls. A ladder led to the one big attic room upstairs, where as many as 12 children might sleep.

The powerful French monarch Louis XIV encouraged the growth of New France, which he hoped would supply the mother country with valuable resources.

Jean-Baptiste Talon, colonial administrator of New France in the late 17th century, took a personal interest in the lives of the colonists. This watercolor shows him visiting common "habitants" in their home.

Unlike their Puritan neighbors to the south, the French Canadians were not a solemn group. They were so diligent about taking days off to celebrate that Quebec authorities complained they were getting no work done. Community cornhuskings, flaxbeatings (flax plants provide the raw material for cloth fibers), harvest time, and sugaring off (when maple trees were "tapped" for syrup) were festive occasions.

There was remarkable agreement among observers that the colonists were oddly fond of fancy dress and luxury. One contemporary noted that a French Canadian "cuts down on [food] in order to be well dressed."

Few habitants could read or write. Personal accounts of their lives are virtually nonexistent. Observers spoke at length *about* them, however. The picture that emerges from their descriptions is of a hardy, brave, vigorous, and sociable people, proud of their new nationality. They skated, tobogganed, or went for sleigh rides in winter. In summer they hunted, fished, and canoed. A Swedish botanist who kept a journal while traveling through French and British colonies in the 1740s noticed that "even the ordinary man surpasses in politeness by far those people who live in these English provinces." This same traveler was also impressed by the religious devotion of the French Canadians, who prayed "more than commonly."

If the habitants left almost no record of themselves, the same cannot be said of the nuns and clergy. Marie de L'Incarnation, one of the first group of nuns to emigrate to New France in 1639, wrote, by one estimate, 20,000 letters home.

This unusual woman left her home in France for an unknown world at the age of 39, after a dream in which she envisioned herself standing in the Canadian wilderness (which she had never visited) alongside the Virgin Mary. A widow and a mother, Marie took her vows as a nun when she felt God had called her to service, even though it meant leaving behind her much beloved 11-year-old son.

Marie de L'Incarnation chanced the voyage to Quebec and founded a school for young girls, Indian as well as French. The nuns there taught the Bible, reading, writing, singing, needlework, and "everything that a girl should know." The staff met with severe hardships. On winter nights, Marie and the sisters slept in beds that closed up like cupboards to keep out the bitter cold; sometimes they wore shoes to bed to keep their feet warm. She tended sick and dying Indians during smallpox epidemics; she watched a large new convent school that had taken years to build burn to the ground in one night. With great difficulty she taught herself the complicated Indian tongues and eventually compiled several small French-Indian dictionaries.

At the outset of her mission, Marie de L'Incarnation had dreamed of bringing God to the Indians, but it was often a frustrating task. "It is a very difficult thing, not to say impossible, to make the little savages French or civilized," she wrote after 30 years in the colony. "We find gentleness and intelligence in these girls but, when we are least expecting it, they climb over our wall and go off to run with their kinsmen in the woods, finding

Riders approach Quebec City's first Ursuline convent. Built in 1642, it burned to the ground in 1650.

French missionaries converted many Indians, including this young woman, who wears a nun's habit.

more to please them there than in all . . . of our French houses."

Marie de L'Incarnation proved influential in the small community, and many of its leading figures valued her advice. They visited her and she conversed with them through a latticework grill (her vows did not allow her to deal directly with men). At age 72 she died in Quebec.

Other fascinating tales of New France were related by priests of the Jesuit order who lived among the Indians as missionaries. Clad in their long robes, wearing only wooden sandals on their feet, priests traveled hundreds of miles through mud and tangled undergrowth to reach the homes of the Indians. For these men, used to the comforts of 17th-century Europe, the Indian manner of living was a severe trial, but they bravely adapted to it.

Like the Indians, the priests lived in flimsy bark "lodges," even in subzero temperatures. Conditions were daunting. The missionary "eats from [a dish] that is very seldom clean or washed, and in most cases is wiped with a greasy piece of skin, or is licked by the dogs," wrote one priest. "The savages' shoes, or the dogs' hairy skins, serve him as napkins, as the hair of the Savage men and women serves them. . . . The meat [is] often covered with moosehairs or sand." In the winters, priests nearly starved. One priest grew so hungry that "[he] went about through the woods, biting the ends of branches, and gnawing the more tender bark."

Worst of all, sometimes, were small annoyances. One priest making a summer trip to Indian country had to pause in the journey because the boat's pilot was injured. Bloodthirsty mosquitos swarmed on the river, and dealing with them was "a task . . . more difficult than facing death itself"—a complaint echoed by many Canadian settlers. The Jesuits considered these trials justified only if they succeeded in baptizing and converting the Indians to Catholicism, which was no mean feat. Tribes often greeted the missionaries, who wanted to take their beliefs away and substitute a foreign god, with suspicion and mistrust. The Indians played tricks on them, tried to lose them in the woods, or stole their meager belongings. Often they believed the missionaries were evil sorcerers, and they eyed askance their strange contraptions—such as clocks or magnifying glasses—and the mysterious marks they made on paper (the Indian tribes had no written language).

Sometimes the tribulations that the fathers endured were almost funny. One missionary complained that when the priests tried to learn the Indians' language, the Indians would substitute "vulgar words" in place of real meanings, which "we would innocently go about preaching as inspiring truths of the Bible." Another had to endure a constant barrage of insults from the tribe: "He looks like a dog! He looks like a bear! He is bearded like a rabbit! He has a head like a pumpkin!"

But the priests persisted, building chapels of bark in the depths of the forest and decorating them with religious paintings or relics they had brought with them. They were willing to go almost anywhere, even among the Iroquois, to win converts.

Back in the solidly Catholic Quebec colony, priests and bishops tried to control the settlers' morals to a degree outsiders found astonishing. One visitor noted that the priests were so zealous that they pulled people away from the dinner table and forced them to attend confession.

But this strong force in the colony was at loggerheads with another equally strong force. The clergy railed against the vices that arose from the fur trade—yet the trade was the colony's chief economic support. The clergy wanted to "civilize" the Indians—to colonize and educate them like the French. The fur trade, on the other hand, required that Indians (as well as some of the French) continue their wild, forest existence—which plenty of French lads were eager to do. It was illegal to trade furs without government-issued licenses, but young men seeking adventure and profit did not care. They were willing to risk anything to become outlaw coureurs de bois.

Voyageurs *paddle a canoe near Ft. William, a trading post situated on the Hudson Bay in the province of Ontario.*

The daring of these backwoodsmen contradicted the conventional view of French Canadians as traditional, home-loving people wrapped in their own provincial world to the point of narrow-mindedness. But 200 and 300 years ago, these people roamed across vast areas of North America, opening up new territory to Europeans. In the United States alone, 3,000 place names are French, and French-named towns are sprinkled throughout Canada.

In many instances these rovers were simply ranging farther and farther afield, searching for furs. In their wake, trading posts sprang up, wooden forts where the men wintered in safety, mingled with the Indians, took Indian wives, and dressed in a strange mixture of French and Indian garb quite startling to the colonists back in Quebec.

Eventually New France held claim to an arc of territory stretching from Quebec down to southern Louisiana. Thus, many American cities began as fur-trading posts, and their post-Indian heritage is French-Canadian. Detroit, Michigan; St. Paul, Minnesota; Milwaukee and Green Bay, Wisconsin; Chicago, Illinois; and New Orleans, Louisiana, are a few such places.

As the fur trade came to be controlled more and more by large companies, the illicit coureurs de bois evolved into "respectable" voyageurs, skilled canoeists whom merchants and companies hired to retrieve furs from the wilderness. The voyageurs' flimsy birchbark canoes, tricky to pilot, were the fastest means of travel in the days before railroads and highways.

The work these men did was not easy. The casualty rate—caused by drowning, Indian attack, illness, or other means—was high. On their voyages, which sometimes covered thousands of miles, the men paddled up to 18 hours a day, sleeping only a few hours at night, and often eating just 2 meals a day. To while away the long hours on their journeys, they told stories or sang as they paddled. Many hundreds of their folksongs have been preserved; some are still sung today. To fit into the canoes, voyageurs had to be short—ideally no taller than five feet six inches. They dressed in red caps trimmed with ostrich feathers, blue hooded jackets, bright sashes, and deerskin leggings. Often they bore scars of their travels, such as half a nose bitten off fighting an Indian or an angry bear.

The voyageurs proved invaluable as guides, leading explorers—French and English alike—into the continent along North America's extensive network of rivers. Long after Champlain's day, the search for a water passage to China was a prime inspiration to men eager for adventure. One such was Jean Nicolet, who in 1634 set out from Quebec. He was so convinced he would arrive in China that he packed a robe of Chinese silk in order to be well dressed when he arrived. Instead of China, he found the present-day state of Wisconsin. A century later, still hoping to discover the western water route, Louis-Joseph Gaultier de La Vérendrye became the first European to see the Bighorn Mountains of Wyoming.

The most famous French-Canadian explorer was René-Robert Cavelier de La Salle. In 1666 he left the priesthood in France for the more adventurous life of a Montreal fur trader and overcame unimaginable difficulties on a journey of exploration across thousands of miles to the Gulf of Mexico. By April 1682, when he

A drawing from 1851 shows the typical voyageur. His cloth cap is blue and decorated with wolf tails.

reached his goal, he and his men had nothing but alligators and potatoes to eat, but he claimed the new land, Louisiana, in the name of the French king. Three years later, returning in an unsuccessful attempt to colonize the area, La Salle missed his mark and landed in Texas. After spending two years lost in the wilderness, he was shot and killed by several frustrated followers.

The period before the mid-1700s has been called French Canada's golden age. It was a relatively short period but had a far-reaching impact: Many of its ways of life continued into the 20th century. The seigneurial system, for instance, persisted until the mid-1800s, and even after that time the habitants' lives still revolved

Voyageurs often had to portage (shoulder their canoes) for long overland stretches during their journeys into fur country. Here a party begins the arduous overland trek.

An expedition led by René-Robert Cavelier de La Salle crosses a frozen Lake Michigan in December 1681.

very much around the villages that grew out of the seigneuries. There, as in the colony's early history, the village, or parish, priests wielded great influence over their flock. Schools were Catholic; priests shaped morality.

Rural habits long held sway in French Canada. People enjoyed the same amusements and customs. ("The fiddler," says Jean Trudel, a writer, remains "the most important figure" wherever tradition has a strong hold in Quebec.) Crafts—such as the needlework and embroidery done by the early nuns of Quebec or furniture making and leatherwork—survived into the 20th century. Until quite recently, extremely large families remained typical in Quebec—a legacy of Louis XIV's reign. Another legacy was the long-standing French-Canadian pride in self. Colonial visitors sometimes interpreted this pride as conceit. But without it, French Canada might never have survived the next crucial episode of its history. ❧

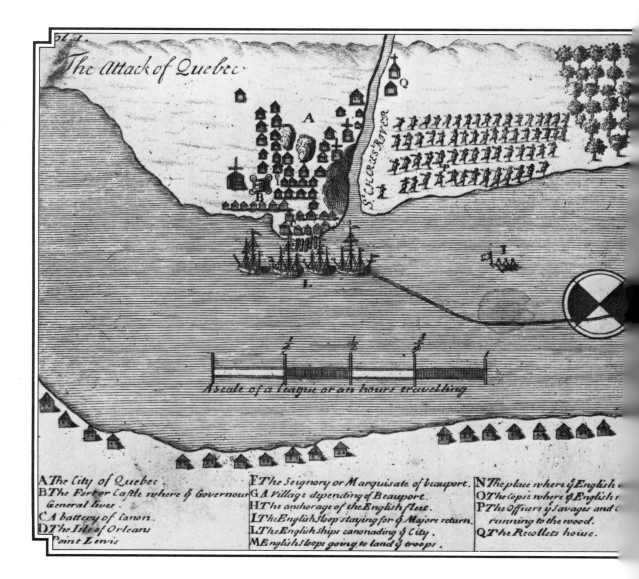

The Attack of Quebec

St. CHARLES RIVER

A scale of a league or an hours travelling

A The City of Quebec.
B The Fort or Castle where ye Governour
    General lives.
C A battery of Canon.
D The Isle of Orleans
    Point Lewis

F The Seignory or Marquisate of beauport.
G A Village depending of Beauport.
H The anchorage of the English fleet.
I The English Sloop staying for ye Majors return.
L The English ships canonading ye City.
M English Sloops going to land ye troops.

N The place where ye English
O The copse where ye English
P The Officers ye Savages and
    running to the wood.
Q The Recollets house.

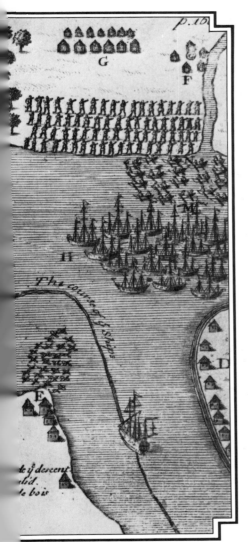

A woodcut from 1703 shows an unsuccessful attack on Quebec mounted by the British in 1690, one of many early skirmishes that pitted the two European powers against each other in North America.

ON THE PLAINS OF ABRAHAM

Today we take for granted that in most parts of Canada, English is the language most widely spoken and understood and that English traditions dominate the land. But French could well have become the national language of the country, and the customs and culture associated today mainly with Quebec or Acadia could well have been those of the entire country.

Canada would probably be very different if the French had won the War of Conquest—otherwise known as the French and Indian War. In retrospect the outcome of this struggle seems inevitable. French colonists were outnumbered by British 20 to 1 (about 65,000 French versus 1.5 million British colonists). Yet until the war was finally decided in 1760, either side stood a strong chance of winning, mainly because the French had an attitude that served them well. As one brash officer put it, "Two thousand [Canadians] will at all times and in all places thrash the entire people of New England."

British soldiers force Acadians, who lived peacefully in Nova Scotia, to swear loyalty to the British Crown.

The French-English feud in North America dated from the early 1600s, when the English sacked Acadia and carried off French prisoners. As time passed and the French spread southward from Canada, down to Louisiana, they collided with British colonists moving westward. Dependent on the fur trade for survival, the French objected to the British trying to make a profit on hunting and trading in territory New France had already claimed.

It was this conflict that in 1754 sparked the ultimate battle for North America. The French had begun building a series of forts in the fur-rich Ohio Valley. From the Virginia colony, which had its own claims in the area, a 22-year-old army officer named George Washington was sent to teach the French Canadians a lesson. After two confrontations, however, he was forced to surrender. Within the year, England sent over troops for a counterattack on the French forts, but again the French defeated them in battle, losing just 24 men, compared to 600 British soldiers killed.

Infuriated, the British in 1755 began driving the French Acadians out of their homes and towns at bayonet point. Much of the hotly contested coastal region of Acadia had fallen into British hands in 1713. French colonists had continued to live peacefully in Nova Scotia, however, refusing only to swear allegiance to the British Crown. Now their rulers, with no provocation, were deporting them to widely scattered and unfamiliar regions, tearing whole families apart. It was a cruel act, and it drove all the French to fight more vigorously.

A good many Indian tribes fought for the French side, even some Iroquois, who at first believed the French would win. These fierce allies helped an army that had already become skilled in Indian fighting tactics, and the French conducted a campaign of deadly raids. In New York, Pennsylvania, Virginia, the Carolinas, and Maryland, the pro-British colonists lived in terror of sudden attack.

"In New France," historian W. J. Eccles has written, "there was jubilation and the sweet heady smell of

victory; in the English colonies, nothing but defeat, cries of woe and rage." Even observers in England thought the British would have to make peace on French terms.

But eventually the tide began to turn. Both France and England sent troops and supplies to their colonies, but France did not match England's expenditures. Even in the best of times, the French crown showed little interest in its colony. And in the mid-18th century, it was still staggering under massive debts incurred by the extravagant reign of Louis XIV. When France did send troops and supplies, England blockaded their entry with its superior naval forces.

In 1758 the French lost several forts in Quebec to the British, and the Iroquois defected as allies. Crop failure and an epidemic brought over in troop ships further strained French resources. Montreal and Quebec City were filled with the ill and dying. Colonists were rationed down to a daily diet of bread and horse meat. Some ate grass.

In June 1759 Quebec was besieged after an enormous fleet of ships and troops sailed up the St. Lawrence. Old men of 80 and boys as young as 12 signed up to defend Quebec. The British infantry was commanded by Major-General James Wolfe, who had sworn to conquer the "Canadian vermin." He suffered from extremely poor health and knew the taking of Quebec would probably be his final act.

Deportation scattered Acadians throughout North America, an outrage that strengthened the will of the French Canadians in the War of Conquest.

Opposing him was a French nobleman, Lieutenant-General Louis-Joseph de Montcalm, who had come from France to take over as troop field commander in 1756. Short, stout, easily angered, he was nonetheless brave and gallant. While Wolfe laid siege to Quebec, Montcalm simply sat back and held on. The city was unusually well placed to withstand a siege, built as it was on 200- and 300-foot-high cliffs above the St. Lawrence and barricaded behind stone walls. Montcalm knew that if he could wait out Wolfe, the British commander would have to get his ships out before the river froze over.

Wolfe was unable to capture Quebec, but he wreaked havoc on the city, bombarding it with cannon fire. "Not a single house without a hole in it," reported an inhabitant of the shell-shocked town. Wolfe also ordered his troops to plunder and burn the outlying countryside. Yet, by September 1759 the city had not fallen and the river had almost frozen over. To mount an assault on the town would mean breaking through ranks of French troops stationed on either side of the city.

It is not clear whether luck or a French traitor led Wolfe to discover a spot about two miles above Quebec, well inside the line of troops, where the cliffs barely

In 1770, Benjamin West—an American who emigrated to England—painted The Death of General Wolfe, *a dramatic rendering of the English general's last gasp on the Plains of Abraham.*

sloped enough to be climbed, a feat Montcalm thought could not be accomplished. The story goes that when the governor of Quebec suggested he put a substantial guard force at that spot, Montcalm wrote him back, "Only God, sir, can do the impossible . . . and we cannot believe the enemy have wings that would allow them in one night to cross water, land, climb rugged slopes, and scale walls."

Montcalm was a poor fortune-teller. At 2:00 A.M. on September 13, 1759, a long line of English boats rowed quietly through the dark to the path on the cliffs. A soldier who spoke perfect French deceived the sentries who challenged the boats, and at dawn, 4,500 men stood outside the city walls on the now storied Plains of Abraham.

Roused by an alarm, Montcalm scraped his army together and hastily rode to do battle. The well-prepared British troops put the disorganized French to flight in a matter of minutes. Both Wolfe and Montcalm were mortally wounded. Told by a doctor that his death was near, Montcalm responded, "So much the better. I shall not live to see the fall of Quebec." It is said that in his last hours, when he was carried bleeding from the battlefield into the city, two women recognized him and began to wail at the sight. More concerned for them than for himself, he reassured them, "It is nothing, please don't upset yourselves," though he knew his wounds were fatal.

By spring France was suffering defeat in Europe as well. In February 1763 France formally gave up control of Canada to Britain. Today, statues of Wolfe and Montcalm stand on the Plains of Abraham. It is unusual for victor and vanquished to be memorialized together. But in this case, "unification" is an appropriate symbol for a nation that has been struggling since the conquest to integrate two very different nationalities.

British merchants and officials moved into Quebec quickly after the war to seize the reigns of colonial wealth and power. Most wanted to bar the French Canadians from holding political office and prevent them

In 1759, General Louis-Joseph de Montcalm died in a doomed attempt to hold British forces at bay during the siege of Quebec.

This woodcut shows English infantry and ships mounting their fateful assault on Quebec.

from taking advantage of any business or commercial opportunities.

As the urban centers of Quebec became more and more anglicized—between 1831 and 1861 there were more English speakers than there were French speakers in Montreal—the French were pushed back into a rural, hardscrabble existence. To all appearances, a sort of French-Canadian Dark Ages began, worsened by the superior attitude of the British. An English woman spoke for many of her compatriots when she described the French-Canadian habitants as "ignorant, lazy, dirty, and stupid beyond all belief."

Like many minorities perceived as inferior, the French were slow to develop an artistic or intellectual culture or nationally known heroes. On average they were less educated than their British and American neighbors. They seemed doomed to fade away as a race, to be absorbed by the dominant culture and then forgotten. Yet against all odds this ethnic group survived as a distinct nationality. It did not simply blend in with the larger society and disappear.

The reasons were several: First, the numbers of the British in Canada were initially low. England had planned on colonists from the south flooding into the new territory after the conquest, but few were eager to move in among this "foreign" people. When British immigration to Canada began to surge in about 1815, most immigrants settled outside of Quebec, in present-day Ontario.

Another factor was the tradition of large families, begun under Louis XIV, which put the population in Quebec at more than 200,000 by the early 1800s. And

(continued on page 57)

LABOR AND LEISURE

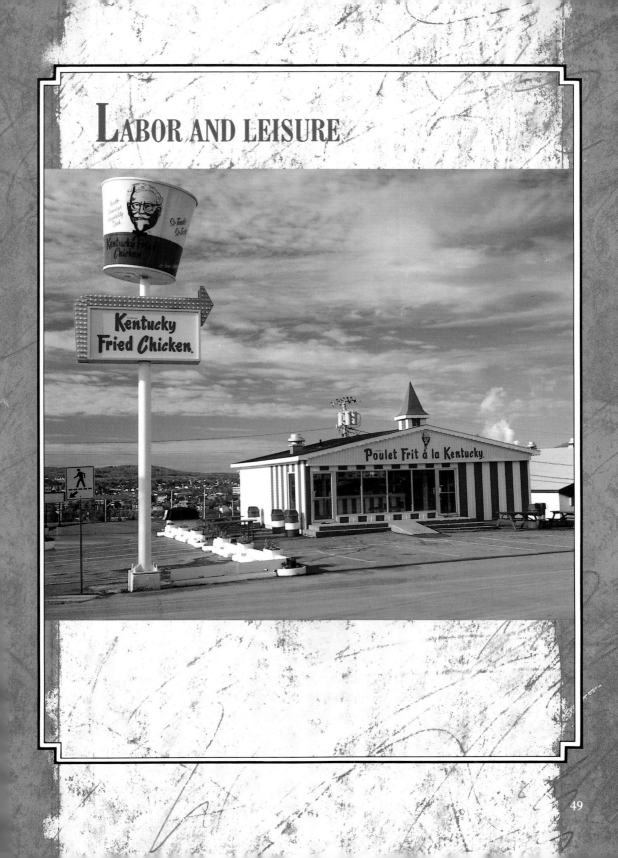

(Overleaf) A Kentucky Fried Chicken franchise in New Brunswick stands as testimony to the influence of American commerce and technology in French-speaking Canada. Despite this infiltration of American culture, French Canadians maintain a deep sense of pride in their own heritage and many enter occupations traditional to the region, such as fishing (top left) and farming (bottom left). No individual more typifies French Canada than the fur trapper, such as the one at right standing by the shores of Lac Saint-Jean in Quebec.

Canadians use their country's many lakes and rivers for work and for leisure. A group prepares to navigate the Jacques Cartier River (top left), rafters ride the white-water rapids of the Outauais (lower left), and fishermen hook the first catch of the day from a lake in Quebec.

*French Canadians reaffirm their cultural heritage through community
festivals and fetes. A crowd enjoys a circus performance and parade at Baie
Saint Paul (above). A group of children marches in the St. Jean Baptiste
Parade in Quebec (bottom right). The fleur-de-lis design on their shirts
represents the iris, a symbol of France since the Middle Ages.*

A young girl and her companion examine fresh strawberries at an outdoor market in Île d'Orléans.

(continued from page 48)

the French tended to marry other French; intermarriage with outside nationalities was considered "a crime against God and a natural abomination."

When, after the conquest, a leaderless people looked to their priests for guidance, the clergy encouraged them to cling to old ways, shunning outside influences that could weaken the pull of Catholicism. This policy has been much criticized for hindering progress and development in French society compared with many other groups in North America, but it did hold French Canada together.

Sheer stubbornness and French pride in heritage were also important to the notion of *la survivance*, or survival, a concept that became a watchword to the people through generations. *La survivance* meant being on guard against anything that threatened language, faith, and traditions. In the years after the conquest, many aspects of Quebec would change—its boundaries, its government, even its name. The steadfastness of its people, however, did not.

Luckily, the British takeover of French Canada was not a complete tragedy. The first two governor-generals in Quebec, although appointed by the British Crown, showed sympathy to the Canadian French. Both assisted in the passage by the British Parliament of the Quebec Act of 1774. This legislation guaranteed the French the right to practice their own religion and guarded much of their custom and law from outside interference.

Under British rule, the French also gradually won a system of representative government, something they had lacked under the rigid rule of the French kings. These strategic concessions were the result of a bargaining chip that the French often found useful in their dealings with the British: England feared that if Quebec was dissatisfied enough, it might join forces with the American colonies to the south.

There was ample cause for British alarm. In 1774 the American colonies were on the brink of a revolution that would lead to their freedom from British control.

Louis-Joseph Papineau, shown here in 1852, was the first French-Canadian statesman to rise to prominence after the English conquest.

American representatives urged Quebec to join them: "Your province is the only link that is wanting to complete the bright, strong chain of union," read one such invitation. Had Quebec leaders responded eagerly, eastern Canada might today be part of the United States.

But the war-weary French were, on the whole, unenthusiastic about the American cause. Many clergymen and members of the upper class actually sided with the British. In 1775, American troops marched on Montreal and Quebec City with the intention of seizing by force what they could not take by persuasion. They were soundly defeated.

Canada had less success staving off the invasion of American ideas. The democratic experiment under way across the border infected French Canadians with the desire for greater political freedom. The British government responded by taking steps to give Canadians an increased voice in government and by creating an elected assembly in 1791. By this time, Canada was spread out too far to be represented efficiently by only one elected body, so the country was formally split in two. "Upper Canada"—present-day Ontario—included a majority of English speakers who had migrated to Canada; "Lower Canada"—Quebec—was mainly French.

In place of the explorers, coureurs de bois, nuns, and missionaries, less colorful but no less necessary figures now arose to direct Canada's future. These were the politicians who struggled over the years to broaden French-Canadian influence in government, education, and the economy. In their wake came journalists who argued and opined about the issues in French-Canadian newspapers, which were plentiful and vocal in the ensuing years.

Louis-Joseph Papineau, an assemblyman and lawyer, was the first French-Canadian leader to become well known after the conquest. Papineau was physically imposing and a golden-tongued orator possessing an eagle-eyed gaze. He led the People's Rebellion of 1837, when the frustrated and impoverished inhabitants of Lower Canada (and also oppressed Anglos in Toronto) rose violently against the British rulers who were oppressing them.

Following this outburst, the British government sent the diplomat and politician Lord Durham overseas to evaluate Canada's troubled situation. His report proved pivotal in the history of both French and British Canadians. Durham characterized the French in terms they would never forget. He called them "uninstructed, inactive, unprogressive," and victims of "hopeless inferiority." The French were outraged, and Durham's language provided a major incentive to keep ethnic pride alive.

English officials agreed with Durham's conclusion that there was "no doubt of the national character which must be given to Lower Canada; it must be that of the British Empire . . . the great race." Thus in 1840 the British reunited Upper and Lower Canada into a giant province, a move meant to drown the Francophone community in a sea of Anglophones. The effect was just the opposite. British Canadians forced to work with the French within the same legislature found they had to compromise to get anything accomplished. French political clout grew.

The reunion of the two provinces foreshadowed things to come. Canadian politicians realized that as a united front, a confederation, the country would gain economically and—of more immediate importance— militarily. As early as 1812, the United States, then at war with England, nearly launched an armed invasion of Quebec. Ever since, Canadians had felt pressure from below the border, as the growing American republic sought to widen its lands. Indeed, until 1920, the top priority of Canadian armed forces was staving off possible American invasion. The best means for maintaining independence seemed to be confederation.

One of the outstanding figures of Canada's "confederacy" years was politician George Étienne Cartier, who understood that the French, instead of resisting unification, should work with British Canadians to secure a place for themselves within the confederacy. He con-

The published opinions of Baron Durham caused a furor among French Canadians and sparked a resurgence of their ethnic pride.

vinced French Canadians of the merits of a confederacy in which each province would control matters of religion, education, and language.

On July 1, 1867 (the date is now a holiday in both French and British Canada), the provinces of Quebec, Ontario, New Brunswick, and Nova Scotia—with the agreement of Britain—joined together as the Dominion of Canada, an essentially self-governing country. Four years later, when British Columbia agreed to join the Dominion, rather than become part of the United States (in good part at Cartier's urging), Canada finally stretched from sea to sea. The French, by that time, formed 31 percent of the total population of the new country.

As the young nation grew, a man who would become the first French Canadian to lead the country at the national level embarked on his political career. Wilfrid Laurier was born in 1841, the son of a Quebec farmer and the descendant of one of the original colonists who founded Montreal in 1642. His parents were not wealthy, but Laurier received a good education. He attended English-speaking schools and grew up fluent in Canada's two tongues. He worked as a lawyer and journalist before entering the Quebec legislature in 1871. Soon he gained a seat in the national parliament.

Dapper, eloquent, and learned, Laurier earned the respect even of opponents, French and English alike. Perhaps because of his bicultural upbringing, less common in that era than it is today, Laurier's chief ambition

This portrait shows the "Fathers of Confederation"—the statesmen, English and French, who forged a unified nation from Canada's various provinces.

was to end the Canadian conflict over race and creed, even if it meant siding with British, rather than French, Canada. To be "simply and above all . . . Canadians" was the ideal he held up to his fellow citizens.

One oft-repeated story about Laurier gives a glimpse of this man's open-mindedness. It seems that the Salvation Army, a vocal Protestant religious organization, came to Quebec seeking converts. As part of its vigorous recruitment campaign, the army paraded through the streets, singing hymns. Angry Catholic leaders wanted to ban the group from the province, but Laurier, though himself a devoted Catholic, would not allow their rights to be violated. "The Army must be allowed to march; if necessary I will march at the head of its procession," he said.

Laurier was elected prime minister of Canada in 1896, a time of nationwide booms in industry and agriculture. "As the 19th century was that of the United States, so, I think, the 20th century shall be filled by Canada," Laurier predicted in a famous remark. When he traveled to England in 1897 to participate in celebrations of Queen Victoria's 60th jubilee, the queen knighted him, raising his (and Canada's) stock worldwide.

Laurier's political career continued even after his 15 years as prime minister ended in 1911, but he presided over rifts between French and British that even his diplomatic efforts could not heal. One ongoing conflict involved the inflammatory question of funding French Catholic schools for the minorities living in largely British provinces. The French sought the same public subsidy for such schools that the British had for their own private institutions. English-speaking Canadians fought them tooth and nail and launched vicious campaigns to block these schools in the Maritime Provinces, in the prairie provinces of Manitoba, Saskatchewan, and Alberta, and in Ontario.

Laurier preferred making a French education available to anyone who wanted it, but he ultimately refused to interfere with a province's right to decide what

Wilfrid Laurier was the first French Canadian to serve as Canada's prime minister. He was elected to that office in 1896 and held it until 1911.

French Canadians often sent their children to Catholic schools instead of to the public institutions favored by Anglo-Canadians. Here, schoolchildren outside St. James Cathedral in Montreal receive the blessings of Cardinal Vannutelli, a papal legate, in 1910.

schools it would fund. Historians remain divided. Some have seen Laurier's gesture as impressively fair; others agreed with the assessment that Laurier "betrayed" the French. At any rate, French language rights outside Quebec increasingly eroded during the years to come.

Laurier also had no solution for the so-called conscription crises, which concerned Canada's responsibility to Britain in time of war and bitterly divided French and British Canadians. Many French saw no reason to fight for a country that was still widely perceived as "the conqueror" rather than as a mother country. In French-Canadian author Gabrielle Roy's classic novel *The Tin Flute*, a character puts the issue this way: "For the last fifteen or twenty years society's never given a damn about us. We were told to make the best of it and shift for ourselves. Then one fine day society falls on our necks. They need us all of a sudden. 'Come and protect us' they cry. . . . What has society given us? Nothing." By nature the French attitude was more isolationist than that of the British Canadians. Political leader Louis-Joseph Papineau himself described his compatriots as "never wanting to go beyond the sound of their own church bells."

When World War I broke out in 1914, Laurier felt Canada should aid Britain, France, and Russia in fighting the rise of Germany and Austria. In 1917, however, when the Canadian government decided to introduce conscription, or the draft, as a means of raising more troops, Laurier warned against it—to no avail. When the conscription act went into effect, riots erupted in

Quebec, and British Canadians made bitter accusations of treason. Young Quebecois men fled to the woods to hide or left the country entirely. Feelings on each side were venomous.

In his seventies, Laurier saw the Canadian unity he had struggled for all his life become even less a reality than when he first took office. When he died in 1919, at 78, he was trying to pick up the pieces after the war and reforge a union between warring Canadian political factions.

During World War II, in the early 1940s, the conscription crisis flared again in Quebec. In this new war—against Germany, Italy, and Japan—French-Canadian voluntary enlistment increased. But when it came to the idea of compulsory service, late in the war, French Canada dug in its heels again. Quebec did not wish to be told by the rest of Canada what it should do. Once again, the two nationalities were polarized and hostile feelings flared. But the close of the war killed the issue before it again became unmanageable.

At the same time, French Canadians who did enlist in World Wars I and II—and there were battalions of French Canadians celebrated for their valor—often were ridiculed by British Canadian soldiers, who mocked their broken English.

On a superficial level, life in Quebec after World War II continued as before. The provincial stereotype of a simple "peasant society" remained unchanged. But as industrialization grew throughout North America, Quebec could not help changing. By 1960, more than two-thirds of the Quebecois lived in metropolitan areas, and the province was an important trade center, exposed to the modernizing influence of the United States.

Meanwhile, the influence of the Catholic church was declining. New currents were at work in Quebec society, although at first they were slow to make themselves felt. The province was like a simmering pot on the stove, bubbling and boiling below the surface. The old ways of thinking would do no longer. After 1960, nothing would be the same again. ❧

French-language recruiting posters helped swell the ranks of Canada's army during World War II.

A crucifix dominates a Franco-American cemetery outside Ft. Kent, Maine.

FRENCH CANADIANS OUTSIDE QUEBEC

Quebec is unquestionably the heartland of French Canada, but French Canada is not confined to the boundaries of one province. The French influence has been felt from the bayous of Louisiana, home of the colorful Cajun culture, to the prairie province of Manitoba, founded by the Metis, a unique European-Indian ethnic group, to northern Maine and the Maritime Provinces, where the Acadians have been a presence for hundreds of years.

French Canadians are scattered through the United States and the Canadian provinces west of Quebec. The 1980 U.S. Census Bureau reported that 780,500 Americans—less than half of 1 percent—claim French-Canadian descent, but broader estimates put the figure at 1.5–5 million. In Canada, outside of Quebec and the Maritimes, the largest percentages of those raised in French-speaking homes currently live in Ontario (4.7 percent of the population), Manitoba (4.3 percent), and Alberta (2 percent).

By far the greatest number of Americans with French-Canadian roots live in New England, close to the Quebec homeland. But many also live in the northern states of Michigan, Washington, Minnesota, Wisconsin, and Illinois. Both Florida and California (interestingly, regions with exceedingly un-Canadian climates) have traditionally had residents of French-Canadian background.

Inevitably, many of the French outside Quebec have blended into the English-speaking culture that surrounds them. There are several reasons for this. Unlike the Quebecois, they often marry outside the group. Ethnically "pure" families disperse because of the pressures of an extremely mobile society. And television, radio, movies, and magazines serve to "Americanize" the younger generations.

At the same time, French-Canadian pride and stubbornness have flourished even outside Quebec. Far from their homeland, French Canadians often clustered in so-called Petits Canadas or Frenchvilles and clung to many of their old ways. They were aided by their clergy, who never failed to nourish the twin flames of language and faith. In the United States and in the Canadian west, as in Quebec, French-Canadian life still

Three seminary students at the Collège des Jésuites of Edmonton, Alberta, wear their hockey uniforms in this 1931 photo.

tended to center around Catholic parishes. An expert on French-Canadian lore recounts tales of priests loading emigrants onto trains and calling out warnings after them: "Lose your language, lose your faith!"

To The Prairies: French Canadians in the West

In 1906, 16-year-old Marcel Durieux left France with his father and older brother for a new life. The family was bankrupt and had decided to start again in western Canada, where farmland was cheap or free for the asking. After crossing the Atlantic on a former cattle ship, packed with other European immigrants, the Durieux family docked in Montreal. Friends there tried to discourage them from heading 2,500 miles west to the unexplored province of Alberta.

They warned "that we wouldn't last," wrote Marcel in his account of his experiences as one of Alberta's first settlers. "Out there, where winters last for eight months, and one can barely harvest potatoes, and where the hail storms are horrible. . . . egg-size. Yes sir! No roads, no bridges."

As young Marcel rode the rails of the newly built Canadian Pacific—the spur that drew more and more settlers from the east to the west—he worried that his cautious friends were right. The train sped through "endless regions of rocks, spruce trees, and lakes . . . the same desert of rocks and stunted trees." However, when his family reached their homestead, near Red Deer, Alberta, Marcel wrote, "[I] froze in my tracks. . . . Indeed, this was the promised land! My eyes filled with admiration. An immense, limitless panoramic view spread before us."

Marcel and his father raced to build their wooden home before the snows hit. Barely into the cabin, they were blasted with temperatures between 30 and 40 degrees below 0 Fahrenheit. There was little food left, and wood for fuel was buried under house-high drifts of snow.

This French-Canadian couple from Edmonton sit for a wedding portrait in 1910.

Despite a hard winter, they survived until the spring thaw. Madame Durieux sailed from France to join her family in the New World, and together the family enjoyed their first Canadian summer. Marcel wrote, "It seemed as if nature, which had been compressed during five months, wanted to make up for lost time . . . hundreds of birds had come up from the South . . . On the open prairie, flowers of all sorts with soft or bright colors grew everywhere, especially tiger lilies and little bluebells."

Marcel Durieux does not explain how his father chose Alberta, Canada. But at that time, the young confederation was actively encouraging European immigration as a means to develop the country's resources. Settlers poured westward across Manitoba, Saskatchewan, and Alberta, heading for mines, farmland, timberland, and oil fields.

Although immigrants from France and Belgium were among them, the proportional number of French-speakers shrank. By the mid-1800s, French Canadians were permanently outnumbered by non-French. Despite desperate efforts by some French clergy to ensure a Catholic, Francophone presence in the west by promoting colonization there, by 1921, French speakers made up only about 6 percent of the western population.

For a people who placed such a strong emphasis on home and family, the west was often simply too remote. When French did head west, however, the church tried to provide French schooling for children and support for societies to preserve French culture and traditions. By the early 1900s, both Manitoba and Alberta had French-Catholic colleges. As the push for la survivance mounted, enterprising French founded Francophone newspapers and radio stations, despite the protests of some English-speaking Canadians. Towns such as Gravelbourg, Saskatchewan, and Morinville and St. Albert, Alberta, have been strongly influenced by the French. And such cities as Edmonton, Alberta, Winnipeg, Manitoba, and more recently areas around Vancouver, British Columbia, have substantial French sections of town.

French Canadians in New England and the United States

In *The Shadows of the Trees*, a history of French Canadians in New England, author Jacques Ducharme wrote in 1943, "The part that Franco-Americans have played in New England is not a showy one. They are the laborers, the small taxpayers, the privates in the Army, the mill workers, the small merchants, the women clerks in the department stores, all common people. They were not a people destined to lead—not at the beginning."

Four decades later, Franco-Americans—the term for U.S. citizens of French-Canadian extraction—are not simply the "little people" of the United States. The group's members include Olympic gold-medal marathoner Joan Benoit of Maine; novelist Jack Kerouac from Massachusetts, author of *On the Road* (1957); and Congressman Joseph Fernand St. Germain of Rhode Island, a powerful figure in Congress.

Some French Canadians were lured to the United States by the California gold rush of 1850. Others came to farm America's arable lands. Later, they flocked to the manufacturing centers of the Midwest (in 1950 Detroit had more French Canadians than any other large U.S. city). Most often, however, the French headed for New England, where even today many older residents still speak French at home in such towns as Lowell, Massachusetts; Manchester, New Hampshire; and Woonsocket, Rhode Island, or in the rural sections of western Vermont, upper New York State, and southern Maine.

The first major migration south of the Canadian border began during the 1800s, when cotton and wool mills, sawmills, and boot, shoe, and furniture factories

Marathoner Joan Benoit, from Cape Elizabeth, Maine, won a gold medal in the 1984 Olympics.

sprang up across New England. From 1880 until 1895, and again during the Great Depression of the 1930s, French-Canadian immigration to the United States surged; ultimately well over a million French Canadians came to America, although some eventually returned to their country. With farmable land in Quebec already scarce, and with families of 10 and 15 children to be fed and an often turbulent Canadian economy, American prosperity tempted French Canadians across the border.

In America, more hardship awaited these newcomers. Work in mill and factory jobs typically meant 6-day-a-week, 12-hour days—sometimes more. Wages were low: Often a whole family, young children included, toiled just to make ends meet. And because French Canadians accepted such menial employment their neighbors—native-born Americans as well as other immigrants—viewed them with scorn.

In *Quiet Presence*, a book of oral histories furnished by French Canadians in New England, a 91-year-old man recalled, "I started working in the mills when I was 12. . . . The hours were from 6:00 in the morning

In the early 1900s, the Franco-American population of Manchester, New Hampshire, depended for news on the French-language daily l'Avenir national, whose print shop is shown here.

to 6:00 at night, but if you were good, they sometimes let you go out to play before the day was over. I started at 55 cents a day—$3.30 a week. I gave it all to my mother."

Conditions at home and the work place were often crowded and dirty. Illness was rampant and death rates were high. But many French had left difficult lives behind, and at least in America a day's work usually meant cash in hand, unlike a day's work on a Quebec farm. They brought their love of socializing and celebrations to the United States and made the most of the free time they had. By the 1870s, Catholic French-language schools had been established in several parishes; over the years their numbers increased.

Franco-Americans straddled two cultures. They observed American as well as Quebecois holidays. In their Catholic schools, the children studied both American and French-Canadian history, often using texts written in Quebec. But on their own time, children spoke English. By the 1950s, French instruction had been reduced to an hour at the end of the day.

Many French remained at a low socioeconomic and educational level for some time. Often they felt they could not afford to keep their children in school. Yet without an education, Franco-Americans could not hope to become wealthier and more powerful.

Some Americans referred slightingly to the French Canadians as "Canucks" (a corruption of "Canadian"), "Frenchies," or "Frogs." Because the French were willing to work long hours for very low pay, often refusing to join labor unions or to go on strike, they antagonized other workers, including another very patriotic, Catholic immigrant people—Irish Americans. The two ethnic groups often competed for the same factory jobs, which sparked hostility between them. Another point of disagreement was their approach to assimilation. The Irish wanted to blend in quickly and resented the French drawing attention to the Catholic religion by their insistence on separate French-speaking

Factory wages were so low that every able-bodied Franco-American worked, including these young girls, shown inside a textile mill in about 1910.

These Franco-American pioneers built their homestead on Wisconsin's White Earth Indian Reservation in about 1875.

priests and French instruction in schools. The result was that instead of working together to combat prejudice, Irish Americans and Franco-Americans waged a constant battle.

Their reluctance to assimilate created a negative impression among other Americans, who resented that in some cases the French moved to the United States only to earn money enough to establish themselves better in Quebec, where they returned at the first opportunity. In the 1940s and 1950s they lagged behind almost every major ethnic group in their U.S. naturalization rate.

Violent anti-Catholicism in the United States also made the French targets of prejudice. In the mid- and late 1800s and again in the 1920s when the Ku Klux Klan was very active, campaigns were waged against the Catholic church and foreign-language schools.

By the 1930s, a change in immigration laws and the onset of the Great Depression in the United States slowed French immigration to a trickle. In New England this hastened the assimilation process that had already claimed many of the Franco-Americans living in the less concentrated spaces of the Midwest.

Acadians

Beginning in 1755, during the Seven Years War, the British expelled about three-quarters of the Acadian population from their homeland in Nova Scotia on the grounds that they posed a threat to British inhabitants of the Maritimes. In fact, the Acadians had remained neutral during the French-British conflicts. Over an 8-year period, perhaps 9,000 to 10,000 Acadians were expelled, a tragedy that became known as the "Great Disruption." A British officer ordered to drive out the Acadians and burn their villages wrote, "It hurts me to hear [the Acadians'] weepings and wailings and gnashings of teeth. . . . [This is] the worst piece of service that ever I was in."

When this trial came upon them, the bulk of Acadians were living quietly in Nova Scotia, farming, fishing, trading furs, and tending apple orchards. They lived harmoniously with Indians in the region; like the people of Quebec, they believed in large families and were devout Catholics. But isolated from Quebec, a difficult two weeks' journey away, and with a different dialect and different traditions, the Acadians considered themselves different from the mainland French.

By all accounts they were a peaceful, industrious, self-sufficient, sociable people. "The inhabitants of the

In this dramatic engraving, British soldiers drag an Acadian away from his family as they are evicted from their homeland.

province," in one nostalgic deportee's words, "seemed to form one single family." And indeed, most Acadians were descended from a few hundred original settlers.

The British did not stop at merely driving the Acadians from their homes. To prevent their regrouping and seeking revenge, they shipped them to colonies up and down the east coast, from Maine to Georgia. Others were returned to France (where their descendants can be found in some regions even today). Those not deported from Nova Scotia went into hiding; some sought refuge in Quebec. The Acadians went also to French holdings in the West Indies. In the drastically different tropical climates, their mortality rate was high. Those in the American colonies were persecuted as Catholics and often had difficulty finding work; they had to take ill-paid labor or beg for a living. Many starved to death.

Several thousand Acadians made their way to the French-founded colony of Louisiana. Another group settled on land that is now part of northern Maine— the Madawaska County region—and in the following years French immigrants from Quebec joined them. Today some 20,000 Franco-Americans—many of Acadian descent—live in this area, and French can still be heard there. Traditionally these Franco-Americans earned their living as lumbermen or potato farmers.

After the French defeat in 1760, the British began allowing Acadians to return to their homeland. But because Scottish, German, and British immigrants had begun migrating there after the conquest, returning Acadians found their fertile lands in Nova Scotia al-

Catholic clergymen aboard a fishing boat in New Brunswick.

ready occupied by newcomers. Many then moved to the unsettled woods of northeastern New Brunswick, where today 32 percent of the population claims French as its mother tongue. In 1969 New Brunswick became the country's only officially bilingually administered province (Quebec is strictly francophone). Back in Canada, the Acadians led a furtive existence. They resumed their quiet lives as fishers, loggers, farmers, and small shipbuilders, and they tried to avoid the British completely. By 1900, 139,000 of them lived in the Maritimes.

The publication in 1841 of Henry Wadsworth Longfellow's romantic poem *Evangeline*, the story of two lovers separated in the Acadian deportations, stirred interest in this unique population and marked the beginning of an Acadian awakening. With a renewed sense of pride, in the 1880s the Acadians chose their own national anthem, flag, and holiday (August 15). They founded French-language newspapers and fought for French-language schools, both of which exist today in the Acadian communities of western Prince Edward Island and Nova Scotia as well as in the larger community in New Brunswick. These communities also

French Canadians in New Brunswick play an informal game of hockey, Canada's national sport.

Many of Maine's Franco-Americans work as potato farmers. Here a farm family (shown in 1942) enjoys their dinner.

hold yearly Acadian festivals and profit from a healthy tourist trade that includes exhibits and reconstructions of Acadian history and restaurants that serve local specialties like *poutine râpé* (grated potato and pork balls.)

Acadians still consider themselves a breed apart from the Quebec French and were long unsympathetic to the Quebecois Separatists' bid. In the past several decades, however, they have more actively demanded recognition for their own culture and language. In the 1960s they established direct cultural ties with France. And in 1960 Louis Joseph Robichaud became the first Acadian ever elected premier of Quebec. Robichaud made concerted efforts to promote a bicultural province and to increase Acadian access to good jobs and education. In 1963 the first Francophone university outside of Quebec was created in New Brunswick—the University of Moncton in the city of the same name. In all, more than 250,000 people in the Maritimes claim French as their mother tongue.

Currently the Acadian community faces the same problem confronting the rest of the Maritimes: a drain of its human resources, particularly its youth, who find employment and job opportunities limited in these less industrialized, less wealthy provinces. Some are leaving for other parts of Canada, others for the United States.

In the 1980s a revitalization of the Acadian community was signaled by a literary work, this time written by a native Acadian. In 1979 Antonine Maillet, born in Buctouche, New Brunswick, in 1929, became the first French Canadian ever to win Le Prix Goncourt, one of France's highest literary prizes, for her novel *Pelagie*.

While she was growing up, Maillet often heard Acadian storytellers recite anecdotes and folktales of Acadian life spoken in a dialect rooted in the 17th and 18th centuries. But there were no Acadian writers; Acadian was only a spoken language. The budding novelist resolved to rescue her native culture from obscurity in a work of fiction that tackled, in Acadian, the topic of the Great Disruption and its effect on her people. The result was *Pelagie*, the saga of a woman who leads a colorful assortment of uprooted Acadians on a 10-year journey, by oxcart, back to their homeland. When she won her award, Maillet declared, "I have avenged my ancestors, for this prize is accorded to a country, and to the existence of a people."

In 1979, Antonine Maillet's Pelagie *won Le Prix Goncourt for the best novel published in French that year.*

The Cajuns

Writers and historians have spilled much ink trying to answer the question "What is a Cajun?" What began as a heritage of birth and nationality is now really a question of tradition, way of life, even character traits. One authority on the subject, author Revon Reed, a Cajun himself, has tried to discuss what a Cajun is in terms having nothing to do with bloodlines: "[A Cajun] loves Cajun music, Cajun cooking, and Cajun traditions. . . . A Cajun loves fishing and hunting; he loves to farm the earth. . . . A Cajun loves to dance and sing, to drink, to amuse himself telling little stories or playing pranks."

Cajun Ron Guidry— "Louisiana Lightning"—on the mound in 1977, when he helped the Yankees capture the American League pennant.

In recent times, well-known figures of Cajun background have gained their fame in entertainment or "leisure-time" fields. New York Yankees pitcher Ron Guidry, 1978 winner of the coveted Cy Young Award, comes from Lafayette, Louisiana, the heart of Cajun country. Chef Paul Prudhomme, whose internationally known New Orleans restaurant, K-Paul's, and best-selling cookbooks have brought the Cajun cuisine to millions, comes from the town of Opelousas, one of the original Cajun settlements. Clifton Chenier's electric accordion and lively blend of Cajun, blues, and jazz music known as Zydeco has influenced country and rock musicians throughout the country, including American singer Paul Simon.

In the strictest sense, Cajuns are the descendants of the several thousands of deported Acadians who began arriving in the still French colony of Louisiana in 1757. They migrated to this fertile, semitropical spot by several means, sometimes by ship, sometimes overland. Settling west of New Orleans, along the bayous (sluggish, swampy rivers) and the winding banks of the Mississippi, they multiplied and spread; from 35,000 in 1815 their numbers grew to 270,000 by 1880. Today the southern third of Louisiana's parishes (the state name for counties) are considered "Acadiana," or Cajun country.

In the very different new climate, mingling with immigrants of other cultures, including black Africans—many of whom came as slaves—and the American Indians already in the region, Acadian customs began to change. Rather than being assimilated by another ethnic group or by American society, the Cajuns picked up bits and pieces from different nationalities and races, while absorbing many inhabitants of southern Louisiana into their own evolving culture. By the mid-1800s, what one writer calls "a lazy way of saying Acadians" prevailed, and the word had changed to Cajuns.

Far from Canada, the Acadians found new food and learned to cook it differently, especially incorporating black African cooking methods. Their specialties were (and are) highly seasoned foods such as gumbo—a thick African-style seafood or chicken soup; jambalaya—a rice, vegetable, and meat stew with infinite variations; or meats and fish such as squirrel, crawfish, turtle, frogs' legs, and alligator. Because wheat did not grow well in Louisiana the Cajuns grew corn instead and made corn breads—for instance, *couche-couche*, coarse, sweetened meal cooked in a skillet. Boudin, a well-spiced pork sausage, is another specialty, always served at community events and festivals.

Acadians were devout Catholics when they arrived in Louisiana, and today Catholicism still predominates as the Cajun religion. But some Acadians apparently developed at least a passing interest in voodoo, influenced by blacks who came to Louisiana from the West Indies and by the fact that New Orleans had become a voodoo center of sorts. This ritualistic form of worship involves magic charms, animal sacrifice, and a belief in zombies or the "living dead." Some Cajuns also believed in the medicinal and healing powers of sorcerers and female "treaters." Association with such renegade forms of spirituality added to an air of mystery surrounding Cajun culture.

In the debate over just what a Cajun is, it has often been said that knowledge of the Cajun language is an acid test. This unusual tongue—which one writer has aptly called a verbal jambalaya—is a mixture of old-fashioned Acadian French with phrases drawn from languages including German, Spanish, American Indian, African, and, increasingly, English. Some jokingly call Cajun French "Frenglish." Like the Acadian language, it is a spoken rather than a written tongue.

Today, at the most, 25 percent of the estimated 800,000 Cajuns in Louisiana and the several thousand more in southeast Texas can actually speak their mother tongue, and fewer still use it in daily conversation. An attempt in the 1960s and 1970s to revive French in the schools has lost some of its steam—and the language taught was classical French rather than true Cajun.

Chef Paul Prudhomme made Cajun and Creole specialties favorites in many regions of the United States.

Traditional Cajun occupations have involved outdoor work such as fishing and gathering shrimp, oysters, and crawfish; trapping muskrats, otters, and a swamp animal called the nutria for furs; and hunting alligators. Cajuns past and present have also made a living as small farmers, cultivating rice, sweet potatoes, sugar cane, corn, and cotton.

Cajuns have suffered from generally high illiteracy rates that have locked them out of higher-paying jobs and left them dogged by poverty. Until 1944, children were not required to stay in school after age 15; many did not. Many Cajun children who did attend school had unhappy experiences: By the early 1920s, Cajun French was banned from the classroom and children who lapsed into it were frequently ridiculed or punished.

Combating stereotypes and prejudice has been one of the most difficult tasks Cajuns have faced. *Lâche pas*

A Cajun fisherman cools the metal bed of his truck before filling it with the day's catch.

The Roger Aldus Band on stage at the Blue Moon Club in New Iberia, Louisiana. Cajun music has traditionally featured the fiddle and the accordion.

la patate ("Don't drop the potato," their slang phrase for "Never give up") is a common saying. In 1939 a U.S. government report dismissed Cajun life as being "without stability, responsibility, or conventionality" and referred sarcastically to the countrified Cajun ways. Yet at no time have Cajuns all been "swamp dwellers." The numerous Cajuns on the southern Louisiana prairies were among the country's first cattle ranchers (a state industry in which they are still powerful), and some Cajuns also became wealthy rice or sugar plantation owners. By the early 1800s, a 35-mile strip along the winding Mississippi River where Cajuns had built their homes was known as the "Golden Coast." In more

Most Americans associate Mardi Gras with New Orleans, but the holiday is celebrated by Cajuns throughout rural Louisiana.

recent times, the Texas oil boom that began some 50 years ago and the Louisiana boom that followed soon after drew many Cajuns to work in the oil fields and tankers, as well as bringing outsiders into their community. The changes signaled the beginning of an increasingly modern way of life for Cajuns.

Today, people of Cajun background work in all fields and have achieved high educational levels. In the past two decades, Cajuns have shown growing pride in their culture, which continues to fascinate tourists, writers, and other visitors.

One expert on Cajun culture hypothesizes that the ethnic identity and pride of this group will be increasingly rooted in their music, an art and entertainment that has been vital to the community since its beginnings. This alternately joyful and melancholy mixture of musical styles and French lyrics is played with violin, accordion, guitar, and brass. As one Cajun writer and musician has described it, "A Cajun's music . . . is like his own soul."

"We are Metis": Riel and the Canadian West

Hero or villain? Mad or sane? A hundred years after his death, mystery still surrounds Louis Riel, one of the most controversial figures in Canadian history. In

Louis Riel led the Metis in their resistance to the Canadian government, which staked a claim to the colony as part of its Dominion in 1867.

his own day, he split the country into two battling camps, pitting British against French even more bitterly than before. One-eighth Indian and seven-eighths French, Riel was considered a half-breed and he fought for the rights of his people, the so-called children of the fur trade.

These were the Metis, descendants of European traders and their Indian wives. By the early 1800s, thousands of Metis were scattered across the western prairies and down into the United States. A majority were of French background; some had Anglo-Canadian fathers and spoke English. Metis also lived in the Maritimes and, in fact, wherever whites and Indians coexisted. But it was the Metis of the western plains who called themselves a nation (*Bois Brûle*—"burning forest") and allied with the French to preserve their rights in the face of the British Americans.

The story of the Metis is also that of Manitoba, Canada's first western province, which evolved from a Metis settlement—the Red River colony, founded in 1812 on the site of modern day Winnipeg. By 1868 the colony had some 12,000 residents, 10,000 of them Metis.

A lively and independent people, most Metis made their living in the fur trade, as buffalo hunters, or by

Most Metis worked as traders, transporting their goods into America's northern prairie states. Here some Metis rest at an encampment during a journey made in 1858.

trading goods with Americans south of the Canadian border. But in 1867 this self-reliant society was threatened by Canadian confederation. The new federal government sent out surveyors to parcel the territory, ignoring the claims the Metis had to it.

Louis Riel came of pioneering stock: His grandmother, Marie-Anne Lagemodière, was the wife of a voyageur and the first non-Indian woman ever to live in western Canada. Riel was sent to Montreal for schooling. He studied briefly for the priesthood, and at the age of 25 he emerged as a Metis leader, intelligent, bilingual, and a riveting public speaker.

In 1869 Riel led the Metis in a campaign to block the Canadian government from staking its land claims. He had the support of the Catholic clergy, who did not want the west taken over by English-speaking Protes-

This print, which shows the interior of a typical Metis cabin, appeared in the Canadian Illustrated News *in 1874.*

In 1884, after Metis held off Canadian police and volunteer troops, the government rushed reinforcements out west on the Canadian Pacific Railroad.

tants. Using both armed force and negotiation, by spring 1870 they had convinced the government in Ottawa to hear out a committee of delegates with a list of Metis demands. In these, Riel and the colonists asked that the Red River settlement be admitted into the new confederacy as a province, with guarantees of land rights and that the French language and Catholic faith be preserved. In July 1870 the first western province, under the Indian name Manitoba, entered the confederacy.

In the course of his campaign, Riel had ordered the assassination of a member of the opposing forces—a Protestant. Canada's Protestants called for Riel's blood, and he was forced to flee the country. For many years Riel roamed North America, suffering periodically from attacks of mental illness in which he saw visions and heard voices. Always intensely religious, at times he believed himself a prophet of God. Although hospitalized for a while, eventually Riel married a Metis woman and settled in Montana, where he taught school.

In 1884 a delegation of Metis came to Riel. Despite the agreement the Metis had made with the Canadian government 14 years before, white settlers had moved onto their land and forced out at least two-thirds of the Metis within a few years. Cheated out of their land or driven off it, the Metis had headed west to present-day Saskatchewan and Alberta. Once again, the Canadian government wanted to claim this land, and the Metis delegation wanted to know if Riel would help lead a second resistance movement. Riel, in fact, had been waiting for this moment. In Saskatchewan he organized a band of Indians, Metis, and even white settlers into an armed uprising known as the Northwest Rebellion.

This time blood was shed on both sides as the Metis and Indians held off a group of police and volunteer troops until a huge number of government reinforcements were rushed out on the new Canadian Pacific line. The vastly outnumbered Metis were quickly defeated. Riel, captured and tried for treason, was sentenced to hang. He refused to consider an insanity defense, even at the cost of his life.

Back in the eastern provinces, the verdict provoked an uproar. Calling Riel "their brother" in impassioned speeches, the French denounced his conviction as a blow against their race and creed. The British Canadians accused the French of sympathizing with a traitor—although even English listeners were moved when Wilfrid Laurier—then a rising politician, gave a passionate speech in Parliament about the persecution of the Metis.

Despite thousands of pleas from the French that Riel's life be spared, the Canadian prime minister, Sir John A. MacDonald, announced: "He shall hang, though every dog in Quebec bark in his favor." On November 16, 1885, Riel went calmly to his death.

In his wake he left a shattered community, which Metis writer Maria Campbell described in her autobiographical work *Halfbreed*: "leaderless, demoralized, defrauded, exploited, poverty-stricken, their whole way of life destroyed, they were a people without a future. . . . Their way of life was a part of Canada's past and they saw no place in the world around them, for they believed they had nothing to offer."

Pushed to the fringes of white society, most Metis eked out a living as best they could, at poorly paid labor. They lived in conditions of deplorable neglect and destitution, prey to illness and despair. Ashamed of their racial heritage, they often tried to hide their background, no longer feeling the pride Riel once did when he made the simple, much-quoted statement: "We are Metis." Maria Campbell wrote bitterly of a childhood memory in her book: "I never saw my father . . . or any of our men walk with their heads held high before white people."

Metis in western Canada today number an estimated 250,000; throughout Canada there may be 800,000 people who claim part-Indian heritage; in the United States there are Metis in western border states, including Montana. In northern Alberta, on a string of govern-

Louis Riel delivered an impassioned defense of his actions at his trial, held in 1885. He was convicted of treason.

I have devoted my life to my country. If it is necessary for the happiness of my country that I should now soon cease to live, I leave it to the Providence of my God.

Louis Riel.

Louis Riel's last words, written just before he was hanged on November 16, 1885.

ment land grants known as the Metis settlements, some 4,000 Metis have consciously adopted a way of life consistent with their heritage. They live in nonindustrialized surroundings, hunting, fishing, trapping, logging, and farming; speak a Metis dialect; and practice traditional crafts.

The turbulent era of the 1960s proved an eventful one for this ethnic group. As French Canadians agitated for change within Quebec, Metis leaders emerged to demand rights for themselves. In 1972, the Native Council of Canada, which addresses Indian concerns on a federal level, was formed, and, around the same time, many provincial and local associations began working to increase job and educational opportunities for the Metis. In 1982 the Metis were formally recognized as one of Canada's "aboriginal," or native, peoples, a landmark decision in terms of their access to government funding. ✇

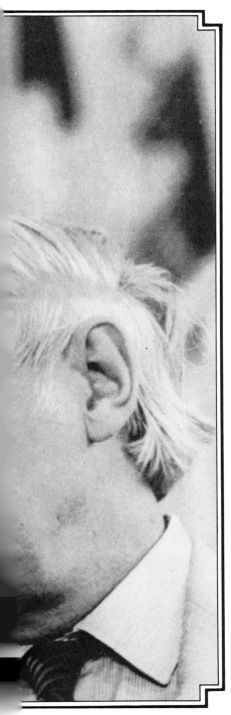

THE QUIET REVOLUTION

In 1911 a young French writer named Louis Hémon visited Quebec and spent several months in rural Lac St. Jean, working on a farm among French-Canadian peasants. Out of his experience came *Maria Chapdelaine*, a novel that became one of the best-known works of Canadian literature.

It tells the story of Maria, a lovely young farm girl who falls in love with the dashing François Paradis, a trapper in the Canadian woods. Her heart is broken, however, when he freezes to death in the wilderness during a blizzard. More suffering follows as Maria's overworked mother dies of a painful, mysterious disease. Tired and heartsore, the girl is tempted to marry another young man who promises to take her away from the harsh life of Canada to a New England city. In a celebrated passage, as Maria tries to decide what to do, she hears the symbolic "voice of Quebec," which persuades her to stay:

> Strangers have surrounded us . . . they have taken into their hands most of the rule; they have gathered to themselves much of the wealth; but in this land of Quebec, nothing has changed. Nor shall anything change, for we are the pledge of it. Concerning ourselves and our destiny, but one duty have we clearly under-

In 1964, during a visit to Quebec City by England's queen Elizabeth, French Separatists staged a public rally.

stood: that we should hold fast—should endure. . . . [W]e are of a race that knows not how to perish. . . . In this land of Quebec naught shall die and naught shall suffer change.

In 1960, as the *La Révolution Tranquille*, or "Quiet Revolution," began, many Quebecois wanted to drown out this voice intoning "naught shall change." The Quiet Revolution referred to the revival of French-Canadian culture and to the wave of political, educational, religious, and economic reform that swept Quebec after the death of staunch traditionalist premier Maurice Duplessis. In 15 years of office, Duplessis had upheld the ideals of religious devotion and peasant values and closed his eyes to the province's crying need for modernization and advances in education. He did not try to force economic control out of Anglophone hands. Thus, French Canadians remained laborers for a ruling—though minority—class of Anglophones.

But a young and growing middle class in Quebec was impatient at being denied the opportunities enjoyed by other North Americans. They were led by such men as Pierre Trudeau, a bilingual, internationally known law professor and journalist, soon to become Canada's prime minister, and by popular television commentator-turned-politician René Lévesque, also bilingual, articulate, and well traveled. "Open the borders! A people is dying from suffocation," cried Trudeau, giving voice to the mounting sense of frustration.

By the mid-1960s, the Catholic church lost its hold on provincial education. Schools and universities began to modernize. Francophones could begin to compete with Anglophones for high-paying jobs.

Suddenly, it seemed, the Quebecois began to exhibit new pride in their ancestry. They sought links with French-speaking countries across the world and renewed long-lost diplomatic and cultural ties with their former mother country. French-Canadian art and literature flourished, giving expression to the people's newfound voice. Books poured off the presses. In 1967, Montreal gloried in playing host to 50 million visitors from around the globe who flocked to Expo '67, Canada's spectacular world's fair.

The Quebec "revolution" was accompanied by a soundtrack, as music inspired the supporters of change, many of whom were young. The *boîtes à chansons*, music clubs still popular in Quebec today, opened their doors to spotlight *chansonniers*—guitar-playing singers—who urged political action or celebrated Quebec life. One of the best-known chansonniers, Gilles Vigneault, wrote a song in 1964 that became virtually an anthem for supporters of change and separatism. "Mon

In 1963, a terrorist bomb decapitated a statue of Queen Liberty, one of Quebec City's public monuments.

pays" (My Country) was his symbolic description of his native land—harsh, troubled, but beautiful:

My country is not a country, it is the winter
My song is not a song, but a gust of wind
My house is not my house, it is the cold
My country is not a country, it is the winter.

Then, seemingly overnight, the Quiet Revolution turned noisy. Frustration pent up over 200 years of British domination came uncorked, and a few members of the movement opted for violence. The *Front de Libération du Québec* (FLQ) carried out a long series of protest bombings, generally in wealthy Anglophone sections of the city.

Gilles Vigneault, a popular chansonnier, *gave voice to the sentiments of the Quebecois.*

Many Quebecois who deplored the violence still wondered if they could ever achieve true equality while remaining part of English-speaking Canada. In 1968 René Lévesque created a new political party, the *Parti Québecois*, with the aim of winning for Quebec more federal funding, wider provincial powers, and legislation to guard French rights and confer equal status. If this attempt failed, Lévesque said, Quebec would be better off without Canada. "It's better to be good neighbors than bad family," he insisted.

A royal commission appointed by the federal government to fully investigate the Anglophone-Francophone conflict warned of "a grave danger for the future of Canada and all Canadians" if the situation was not cleared up, adding that the country was passing through "the greatest crisis in its history." The government acknowledged serious inequities between the two nationalities and tried to redress the balance. It ruled that products packaged in Canada had to be labeled in both French and English. The government gave Quebec greater leeway in choosing how to spend federal funds than other provinces had. Most importantly, in 1969 Canada became officially bilingual: All federal services were made available in French and English, while a costly campaign to teach French to federal government employees began.

Across the country, particularly in the western provinces, rumbles of discontent swelled to roars as other Canadians protested the lengths and expense to which the federal government was going to "humor" Quebec. They were especially displeased at having French "forced down their throats," as the saying went, by the Official Languages Act of 1969, which made both English and French the lawful languages of Canada.

This ambitious attempt to transform Canada into a nation "where both French- and English-speaking Canadians . . . feel at home in all parts of this country," was that of Prime Minister Pierre Trudeau, who took office in 1968. A charismatic man known for trademark touches like the rose in his lapel or impulsive, public

In 1969, French-Canadian demonstrators express their contempt for "Bill 63," which guaranteed Quebec parents the right to send their children to either French- or English-speaking schools.

On October 15, 1970, the Canadian government invoked the War Measures Act in response to the kidnapping of James Cross, a British diplomat, and Pierre Laporte, Quebec's labor minister.

gestures like sliding down a banister, Trudeau was also steely-willed, brilliant, and emphatically not a Separatist. His was a vision of a united Canada where two equal nationalities shared power.

When Trudeau and the radical Separatists clashed head to head, the result was one of the most dramatic and controversial crises of recent Canadian history. The FLQ had grown more and more strident in its actions as the 1960s wore on. "During 1968 we tried to make people understand," the group warned after a bombing. "During 1969 we will kill those who have not understood."

In the fall of 1970 the FLQ kidnapped British diplomat James Cross and a minister in Trudeau's cabinet, Pierre Laporte, from their homes, demanding, among other things, the release of FLQ prisoners jailed for bombings and ransom money. Trudeau would accede to the FLQ's demands, but Laporte was murdered, strangled with the chain of a religious medallion he wore. Cross was released unharmed, however, and the era of terrorism in Quebec drew to a close.

The era of separatism, however, did not, as the province continued to "Frenchify" itself. Previously, Francophones had been forced to learn English if they hoped to advance far in society. Beginning in 1974, a series of language bills in Quebec reversed that situation. French not only became the official tongue of the province, it became the only language that could be used on everything from road signs, shop signs, and billboards to offices and all but a few school classrooms. Use of the English language was not a matter of choice—it was largely illegal. Anglophones within the province first protested and then left in droves; some 100,000 moved out of Quebec during these years.

There was more to come. In 1976 René Lévesque and the Parti Québécois had been elected to power in Quebec in an upset victory that took Lévesque as much as anyone by surprise. He had campaigned on the issue of what he called "Sovereignty-Association" (what everyone else called separatism) for Quebec. This called for Quebec to become politically independent of but economically linked to the rest of Canada. By the late 1970s, it seemed entirely possible that Quebec might secede from Canada.

Trudeau fought Lévesque all the way, insisting separatism would mean economic disaster for Quebec. He promised that if Quebec remained in the Dominion, he would seek to revise the nation's 1867 constitution to weaken provincial powers and make discrimination against minorities illegal; he would also guarantee Quebecois rights through a bill of rights.

But Lévesque proceeded with his plans. By the spring of 1980 he was ready. The Quebec Referendum asked the people of the province to decide at the polls if they wanted to separate from the rest of the country. The outcome of the election was uncertain, and Canada waited tensely for a verdict.

When the Referendum results came in, Lévesque was again surprised—this time unpleasantly. As one politician remarked, in an attempt to explain the voters' decision to uphold allegiance to Canada: "The Canada that Mr. Lévesque wants to separate from no longer exists." By 1980 the people of Quebec were seeing that many of the goals for which they had fought had been achieved. Canada had become increasingly bilingual. As of 1986, some 16 percent of Canadian people spoke both French and English. Schools across the country, at all levels, with the aid of government funding had incorporated more French courses into their curriculums.

René Lévesque (at the microphone) celebrates his election as Quebec's premier in 1976. The sign says We Need a Real Government. It Can't Continue as It Has.

Within Quebec since 1960 a variety of Francophone universities had opened (currently there are 10 in the province). Job opportunities had broadened for both Francophone and bilingual Canadians; French speakers everywhere had access to services and education in their own language. And so, in 1980, the Quebecois said no to separatism. Lévesque would remain in power some years more, but his burning issue was gone. The people had spoken, and the province was entering a new phase of its history.

Even while Quebec was preoccupied with politics, everyday life went on. Along the St. Lawrence, the port city of Montreal has grown into one of North America's most sophisticated metropolises, a lively mecca for film, music, theater, and literature, scarcely fitting the image of French Canada as backward or old-fashioned. With a metropolitan population of almost 3 million, Montreal is often called the world's second largest Francophone city after Paris, although heavy emigration has given it a uniquely multicultural flavor.

Each year more than 5 million visitors flood Montreal. Once there, they are entertained by attractions such as the famous underground city within a city—8 miles of businesses, shops, restaurants, and transportation built beneath the streets and sidewalks, so that people don't have to go outside in the bitter winter weather. Glass and concrete skyscrapers of innovative design tower above the same Mont Royal that Jacques Cartier once climbed, and over Vieux Montréal (Old

On May 20, 1980, Quebecois voted down a proposal to put the province on the road to political independence. At left, an opponent of the measure; at right, René Lévesque.

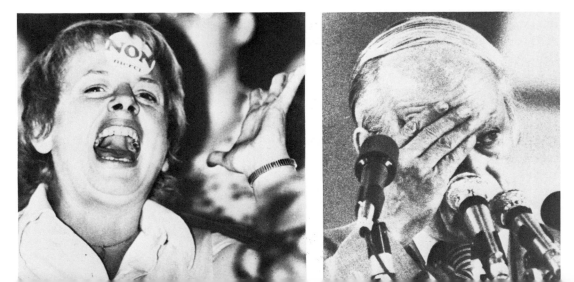

The Montreal skyline in the 1980s. The largest city in Canada, it is also the world's second-largest Francophone city, after Paris.

Montreal) with its narrow, cobbled streets and buildings of old gray stone.

One hundred and seventy miles northeast of Montreal lies quieter Quebec City, its skyline almost unmarked by tall buildings. The provincial capital is more truly French than Montreal: Some 97 percent of the 600,000 residents in greater Quebec City are Francophone. The city has tried to preserve its history intact: Within the larger town, stone fortifications, built both before and after the conquest to keep out invaders, ring a walled city, the only structure of its kind in North America.

Today an elevator carries tourists between the upper and lower town, along the cliffs once scaled by General James Wolfe and his men. For 10 days each February, roughly at the time of the Mardi Gras celebrations in Louisiana, the famous Quebec Winter Carnival, with its parades, sports events, and fantastical ice sculptures of birds, beasts, and palaces, draws thousands of visitors willing to brave the harsh winter weather.

If it is simplistic to say Quebec province's many smaller towns and villages still harbor an unspoiled "peasant" way of life, it is also true that travelers through rural areas such as the wild Gaspé Peninsula— the arm that juts out below the St. Lawrence—will find many spots where only French is spoken and where farmers, fishers, and laborers continue a manner of living their families have known for generations. ❧

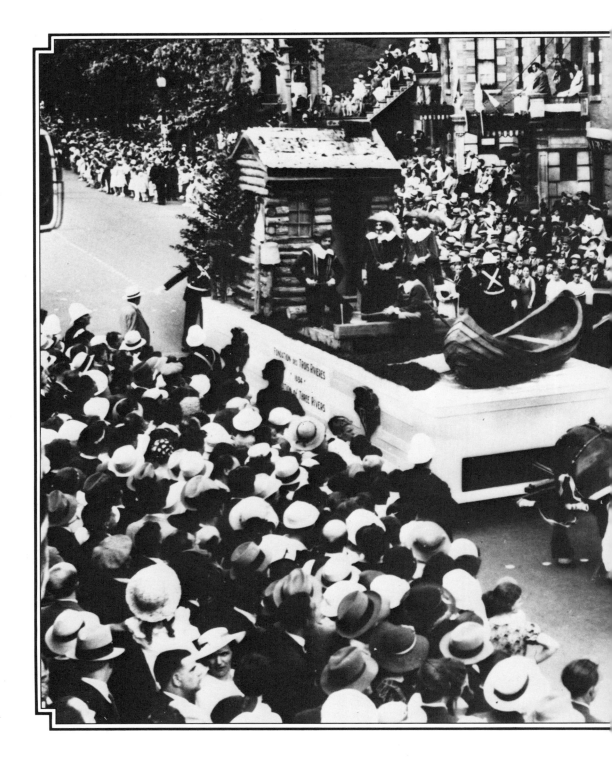

In 1934, the 100th anniversary of the St. Jean-Baptiste Society of Quebec marked a landmark in French-Canadian self-awareness.

FRENCH CANADA IN THE TWENTY-FIRST CENTURY

What will the term "French Canada" mean 100 years from now? Will a unified Francophone culture still exist? What of the French language in North America—can it survive? It's a topic on which opinions vary.

Carole, a social worker living in Montreal, says most of her friends speak only French, but she is nonetheless pessimistic. "When you have to make laws to keep a language, you know you're starting to lose it," she says, referring to the Quebec legislation (challenged in the late 1980s) that limits the use and teaching of English within the province. "We live in North America and this is an English-speaking world. I think the language may be lost."

Girard, a teacher and businessman also living in Montreal, agrees: "Our economy is getting more inter-related with the U.S.'s and is also going towards technology—which is mainly devised in the U.S., in English," he points out. "The dangers of not bothering with French because it won't be practical in everyday life will just increase."

Indeed, the influence of the nearby United States on Quebec cannot be overlooked when considering the issue of assimilation. American culture and the English language continually invade the province not only through technology, but in pervasive forms such as rock music, fast-food chains, movies, and television. "Frenglish" speakers mix languages without thinking twice, saying "Donnez-moi un hamburger" (Give me a hamburger) or referring to "le fun" or "un party."

But many are optimistic about the future of the French culture and tongue in Canada. A French studies professor of Quebec origin, now on the faculty of a university in the United States, comments: "There is no question that the French language will continue to be maintained there. The young people—that's always the way you can tell—if the young people were abandoning the French language in Quebec, you would see the writing on the wall, but that is not what's going on now."

An Anglophone editor who lived in Montreal during the turbulent 1960s and 1970s concurs: "French Canada has seen its worst hour and survived. You won't lose the culture now; it's too strong. There are still little towns along the Saguenay River and the Gaspé Peninsula where the English haven't even made a dent."

However, statisticians and professors who study the Francophone culture point out that Quebec faces two major problems in its fight to maintain its identity. Currently the Francophone birthrate has sunk to a relatively low level. One reason is that a strong women's movement has brought much of Quebec's female population into the workplace. Another is that the Catholic church, which disapproves of birth control, has lost some of its influence.

At the same time immigration into the province, Montreal in particular, is very heavy. Italians, Greeks, Asians, Jews, Germans, Middle Easterners, and many other nationalities now belong to Quebecois culture. In 1988 some 21 percent of Montreal's residents were of neither French nor British origin; although Quebec does attract some French-speaking immigrants—from Europe, Haiti, and Africa—by far the larger percentage is not Francophone. The provincial government has tried to address this situation by requiring, in most cases, that children of immigrants attend French-speaking schools. But there is no way to legislate the language spoken at home.

In French-Canadian communities outside of Quebec, ethnic societies and festivals, newspapers, and broadcast media still foster a sense of heritage and tradition, but inevitably in most of these areas it will be hard for the French to resist the anglophone tide indefinitely. Manitoba and Ottawa, for instance, have both taken major steps toward bilingualism, yet only 5 percent of Manitobans and 13 percent of Ottawans who were raised speaking French now list it as their only language. By contrast, in the province of Quebec, 72 percent of those whose mother tongue is French still claim it as their primary language.

In an era when the media help define a society, there exists a Francophone communications system whose breadth and sophistication are virtually unmatched by any other non-English-speaking group in North America. The Canadian Broadcasting Corporation's French division, Radio Canada, maintains nationwide French television and radio stations that give Francophones across the country access to dramas, news, game shows, sports events, films, and advertising in their own language. (Some is U.S. fare dubbed into French; in the late 1980s, "Dallas" was the most popular TV show exported from America.) French-Canadian radio stations are required to feature French music in 75 percent of their programming.

Montreal alone has three French daily newspapers, and Quebec bookstores do a brisk trade in works imported from France, in translations of English-language best-sellers, and in books by Quebecois writers. Some of these French-Canadian authors are read both in Canada and France. Leading contemporary authors include Michel Tremblay, considered one of the best French-

Author Gabrielle Roy as she appeared in 1964, 19 years after the publication of her masterpiece, The Tin Flute.

language playwrights currently writing, and Mavis Gallant, whose witty stories often grace the pages of the *New Yorker*.

One of the first French-Canadian authors to achieve international stature died only recently in Quebec City, where she had made her home for many years. Gabrielle Roy, author of *The Tin Flute*, was born in Manitoba in 1909, one of 11 children in a poor family. She first entered the working world as a schoolteacher, teaching impoverished Metis children in small villages on the prairies.

In Roy's day it was highly unusual for a woman (especially one who was young and poor) to seek a career as a writer, and it took her years to find the courage to act on her ambition. At 30, Roy moved to Montreal, where she knew no one, and joined the staff of a local newspaper, writing on her own in her spare time. She lived in a small apartment. On one side of her was the wealthy Anglophone section of Montreal; on the other was a French slum. Roy grew deeply disturbed by the economic disparities between the two populations.

The Tin Flute, her acclaimed first novel, tells the story of Florentine, a young French girl who works at the lunch counter in a cheap dime store in order to help support an unemployed father, a patient and long-suffering mother, and several brothers and sisters. Florentine is a fighter, intent on leaving her bleak existence for a more comfortable one—by whatever means available. Roy's unsparing portrait of this girl conveyed the toll poverty takes on the human spirit. It leaves little room for kindness, self-respect, or virtue, and no more chance for happiness than that provided by a dime store trinket (the shiny tin flute of the title).

Published in 1945 and read in Canada, Europe, and the United States, *The Tin Flute* showed readers who had held the vague idea of Quebec province as a land of contented peasant farmers that many Francophones were in fact urban slum dwellers. *The Tin Flute* won prizes and praise, but its author was disappointed by the poor conditions that continued to plague French Canadians. Later works reiterated her concern with the social conditions affecting her people. Luckily, Roy lived long enough to see Quebec take giant strides into the better future she had hoped it would achieve. Gabrielle Roy died in 1983.

Many other French Canadians served as inspirations to their compatriots, even though they did not necessarily share Roy's mission. In fact, one of the proudest offerings of French-Canadian culture is the sport of ice hockey. Little French boys are said to learn how to skate before they can walk, and many youngsters spend long hours playing hockey.

French Canadians have played on every team in the National Hockey League, and since the Quebec City Nordiques formed in 1972, Quebec province has had two professional teams. One of them, the Montreal Canadiens—nicknamed the "Habitants" or "Habs"— had won the Stanley Cup, awarded to the league champions, 23 times as of 1988. One sportswriter has described the team's glory years in the 1950s, 1960s, and 1970s as a "success unmatched, perhaps, in the history of professional sports." The team's stars have included Guy Lafleur, Jean Béliveau and—brightest of them all and a legend among his people—Maurice "Rocket" Richard.

Maurice Richard was born in 1921. By the time he was four, he was skating on the river running through his Montreal neighborhood. When he was 21, he signed a contract with the Canadiens. Quiet and serious, Richard nonetheless had a quick and violent temper, a trait for which he became almost as well known on the ice as he was for his brilliant play. In one memorable Stanley Cup playoff game, Richard practically went into a coma after a Boston Bruin hit him with his stick. Richard stayed on the ice, however, and broke a tie in the final minutes of the match with a shot so miraculous and improbable that a teammate watching him fainted and the home crowd gave him a four-minute ovation, the longest in the Canadiens' history.

In 1955, when Richard was suspended before the Stanley Cup playoffs, again for brawling with two Boston Bruins, angry Montrealers tried to kill Clarence

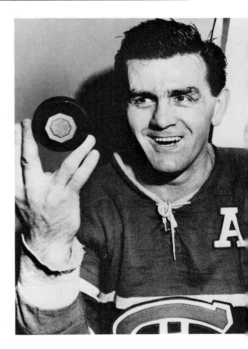

In 1954, Maurice ("the Rocket") Richard celebrated his 400th goal by holding up the puck he scored it with.

An age-old French-Canadian event occurs every spring, when Quebecois head into the woods to draw sap from maple trees.

Campbell, the NHL president who suspended the star. Fans rioted in the streets, overturning cars and newsstands, breaking windows, and looting, ultimately causing an estimated $100,000 worth of damage. This incident is often cited as a pivotal event in what became the "Quiet Revolution."

Hockey is not the only French-Canadian custom that keeps the culture united. So do some long-standing traditions. A holiday such as St. Jean Baptiste Day on June 24—Jean Baptiste has been French Canada's patron saint since the days of New France—is still lavishly celebrated with parties, bonfires, and fireworks. Christmas, particularly in rural areas, is frequently observed as it was a century ago, with the *Réveillon* (midnight supper)—a large dinner of traditional delicacies including *tourtières* (meat pies) and *ragoût* (a kind of stew) served in the wee hours on Christmas Eve, after the family has returned home from midnight mass.

Each spring, when the sap in the maple trees begins to run, the French head off to the woods and their *cabines à sucre* (literally, "cabins for sugar") for the sugaring-off ritual that has become a tourist attraction. Modern-day habitants gather in small family-owned cabins and tap trees for a thin, clear syrup that is then boiled down into thick maple syrup or sugar. As the hot syrup cools, it is poured over trays of snow, where it immediately hardens into maple taffy and is scooped up and devoured by interested onlookers.

If the future of French Canada in years to come remains uncertain, the impact that this ethnic group has already had on Canada is easier to assess—even apart from New France's exploration and settlement of the virgin North American continent.

In the last 25 years, the French have forced Canada, if rather reluctantly, to redefine itself as a nation. The broad revision of the Canadian constitution, only completed in 1987, was in good part a result of Pierre Trudeau's 1980 promise to Quebec that he would reexamine Canada's underlying political framework if the Quebecois rejected separatism.

Agitation by the Quebecois was responsible for the country's adoption of two official languages, and now politicians aspiring to national prominence find it helps to speak two tongues; Prime Minister Brian Mulroney, elected in 1984, was born in Quebec and is fluent in French and English.

The increased attention that the French focused on the issue of discrimination ultimately expanded the opportunities offered to other minority groups. As Pierre Trudeau put it, Canada strove to be "a multicultural country within a bilingual framework."

But perhaps French Canada's most important contribution to the nation is its effect on the Canadian sense of self. Historians and commentators frequently mention the phenomenon of the Canadian "identity crisis," which owes much to the fact that a population approximately one-tenth the size of the United States is spread throughout the second largest country, in terms of area, in the world. With its citizens so geographically scattered, Canada has taken far longer than its southern neighbor to feel like a united nation.

Resentful as they may have been of the French at certain times in their history, Canadians have to admit that without them, the country would be hard put to come out from under the giant shadow cast by the United States. Quebec adds a different thread to the national fabric.

Ian, a British citizen who has lived in Montreal for 20 years, is aware that every guidebook on Quebec uses the same phrase to describe the people but cannot resist saying, "I know it's an old cliche, but it's the truth: there's a 'joie de vivre' [joy in living] in Quebec found nowhere else. The people have style, passion; they're good-natured. I've been totally accepted; if the French think you want to speak their language, they embrace you wholeheartedly. I find Quebec is a constant learning experience." ❧

On April 17, 1982, England's queen Elizabeth signed a proclamation formally granting Canada its independence. Here, she hands the historic pen to Prime Minister Pierre Trudeau.

FURTHER READING

Brault, Gerard. *The French-Canadian Heritage in New England.* Hanover, NH: University Press of New England, 1986.

Durieux, Marcel. *Ordinary Heroes: The Journal of a French Pioneer Family in Alberta.* Edmonton: University of Alberta Press, 1980.

Eccles, W. J. *The Canadian Frontier: 1534–1760.* Albuquerque: University of New Mexico Press, 1983.

Hallowell, Christopher. *People of the Bayou.* New York: Dutton, 1979.

Hemon, Louis. *Maria Chapdelaine.* New York: Macmillan, 1921.

Hendrickson, Dyke. *Quiet Presence: Dramatic, First-Person Accounts—The True Stories of Franco-Americans in New England.* Portland, ME: Guy Gannett Publishing, 1980.

Longfellow, Henry Wadsworth. *Evangeline.* New York: Avon, 1971.

Parkman, Francis. *France and England in North America.* 1865, Reprint. New York: Viking Press, 1983.

Roy, Gabrielle. *The Tin Flute.* New York: Reynal & Hitchcock, 1947.

Thompson, Wayne C. *Canada 1987.* Washington, D.C.: Stryker-Post Publications, 1986.

Wade, Mason. *The French Canadians, 1760–1967.* New York: St. Martin's, 1968.

INDEX

Picture credits

We would like to thank the following sources for providing photographs: A. A. Ayer Collection, Newberry Library: p. 39; Archives Nationales du Quebec, Quebec City: p. 36; Art Resource: p. 33; The Bettmann Archive: (cover), pp. 16, 45, 60, 73; Bettmann Archive/BBC Hulton: p. 61; Canadian Pacific Railroad: p. 86; Canapress Photo Service: pp. 77, 94, 96; Dimond Library, University of New Hampshire: p. 70; Glenbow Archives, Calgary, Alberta: p. 89; Philip Gould: pp. 80, 81, 82; Gouvernement du Quebec: pp. 50, 51, 52, 53, 54, 55, 56; Government of Canada, Regional Industrial Expansion: p. 99; Huntington Library, San Marino, California: pp. 18–19; Library of Congress: pp. 20, 48, 62, 64–65, 76; Minnesota Historical Society: pp. 72, 84; Museum of American Textile History: p. 71; National Archives of Canada: pp. 25, 28, 30, 31, 32, 34, 40, 44, 47, 58, 59, 63, 85, 88, 104; National Gallery of Art, Washington, D.C.: p. 41; National Gallery of Canada, Ottawa: pp. 35, 46; New York Public Library Picture Collection: pp. 21, 26, 47; PAR/NYC: p. 49; Prints Division, New York Public Library: p. 23; Provincial Archives of Alberta: pp. 66, 67; Provincial Archives of New Brunswick: p. 75; Rare Book Division, New York Public Library, Astor, Lenox and Tilden Foundation: pp. 42–43; S.S.C. Photo Centre A.S.C.: pp. 50, 56; Saskatchewan Archives Board: p. 83; Donna Sinisgalli: p. 22; State Historical Society of Wisconsin: p. 38; UPI/Bettmann Newsphotos: pp. 12–13, 14, 15, 69, 78, 79, 90–91, 92, 93, 95, 96, 98, 100–101, 105, 106, 107

NANCY WARTIK is a free-lance writer living in Brooklyn, New York. Formerly head of editorial research at *Ms.* magazine, she has published articles in *Ms.*, the *New York Times Book Review*, and *Venture*. She holds a B.A. in English literature from the University of California, Santa Cruz.

DANIEL PATRICK MOYNIHAN is the senior United States senator from New York. He is also the only person in American history to serve in the cabinets or subcabinets of four successive presidents—Kennedy, Johnson, Nixon, and Ford. Formerly a professor of government at Harvard University, he has written and edited many books, including *Beyond the Melting Pot, Ethnicity: Theory and Experience* (both with Nathan Glazer), *Loyalties,* and *Family and Nation.*